PRIOR **MY BATTLES**
"I CAN'T AFFORD TO FIGHT YOU TOO!"

VISIONARIES
DR. JAQUELYN HADNOT & DR. DEBORAH ALLEN
Foreword: Dr. Joyce Haddon

© 2023 Deborah Allen

Book Cover Design: Nichol LeAnn Perricci, DNP Designs
Interior Book Design & Formatting: TamikaINK.com
Editor: Tee Tunnell Harris| TamikaINK.com

ALL RIGHTS RESERVED. No part of this book may be reproduced in any written, electronic, recording, or photocopying without written permission of the publisher or author. The exception would be in the case of brief quotations embodied in critical articles or reviews and pages where permission is specifically granted by the publisher or author.

LEGAL DISCLAIMER. Although the author has made every effort to ensure that the information in this book was correct at press time, the author does not assume hereby disclaim any liability to any party for loss, damage, or disruption caused by errors or missions, whether such errors or omissions result from negligence, accident, or any other cause.

Published By: Igniting The Flame Publishing

Library of Congress Cataloging-in-Publication Data has been applied for

ISBN: 9798865492801

PRINTED IN THE UNITED STATES OF AMERICA

TABLE OF CONTENTS

Foreword By Dr. Joyce Haddon 5

Prioritizing My Battles By Dr. Jacquie Hadnot 11

I Can't Afford To Fight You Too! By Dr. Deborah Allen 33

Choose Your Battles Wisely: WWJD? (What Would Jesus Do?) By Featured Author, Dr. Pamela Henkel 45

Don't Come For Me; I Didn't Send For You
By Dr. Cindy Betts 59

The Battle Of The Mind By Dr. Phyllis Fuller 77

The Consequence Of Spreading Myself Too Thin, Taking On Too Many Battles By Mary Davis 89

Prioritizing You While on The Frontline of the Battle
By Shanice Murphy 101

Riding Through the Storm By Sandra (Sandy) Johnson ... 113

Balance in the Battle By Dr. Stephanie Gore 123

Getting To Know God By Sarah McLean 139

Stop Fighting Yourself! Get Out of Your Own Way!
By N. Lynn Gobert 153

Prioritizing My Battles: I Cannot Afford to Fight You Too
By Roschelle Taylor 169

Every Battle Is Not Mine By Dr. Janice Grier 179

An Unwavering War By Gwendolyn E. V. Monroe 187

Warfare With Guilt and Shame By Dr. Evelyn Hill 203

Overcoming Adversity By Kellie Knights.......................... 217

Walking Wounded By Muriah Brown.............................. 227

Foreword
By Dr. Joyce Haddon

"All my life I had to fight" was a gut-wrenching confession by Miss Sophia in the iconic movie The Color Purple. This profound confession is reflective of my own testimony, which, for many years, I wore as a badge of honor. Growing up on the north end of Detroit, MI, I was raised in an environment where every day I had to fight to survive. Fighting battles physically, spiritually, mentally, and emotionally that often were not battles of my own.

Somehow the enemy keeps us in a whirlwind of battle, manipulating us into believing that fighting to live, fighting our way to the top, and fighting for what we want is a sustainable pathway to victory. This mindset is counterproductive to the believer because it keeps us out of alignment with the true plan of God for our lives.

Imagine the amount of time, energy, and money wasted engaging in battles, declaring war in areas wherein fact Christ has already granted us victory through His sacrifice on the cross.

This body of work captures the premise of spiritual warfare. It dismantles the plan of the enemy by equipping the reader with strategies to counteract the opposition. Dr. Allen's and Dr. Hadnot's prolific insights challenge the reader to activate their God-given authority in the face of adversity by discerning and prioritizing what battles, if any, warrant our attention.

As you delve into this life-changing compilation, I believe the Holy Spirit will release you from the ungodly need to "attend every fight you're invited to." That you will be healed from the scars of battles fought yesterday and that through this book, your focus will be shifted to the fulfillment of your purpose.

Dr. Joyce Ruth Haddon

Dr. Joyce Ruth Haddon was born in Fort Bragg, North Carolina. She was the 6th of 8 children. Dr. Haddon was known in her community as "trouble." It was predicted she would be found in an alley because of her lifestyle. She was, to many, a lost hope and was considered a "nobody," and she would never amount to anything. However, she had a praying mother. Her mother would often say, "I prayed until I was satisfied."

Dr. Haddon preached her first sermon in 1968. Dr. Haddon holds two Honorary Doctorates: from Tuskegee University in Tuskegee, Alabama, and from Next Dimension University in Ontario, California.

As a young woman, Dr. Haddon found herself in a domestic violence relationship and was beaten and dragged through the streets of Detroit, openly humiliated, and left to die. During the process of separation and divorce, she would find herself homeless and living in her sister's basement. The gift of prophecy rests heavily upon Dr. Haddon, as many have testified of the accuracy of the prophetic words that they have received through her ministry.

Dr. Haddon's testimony has allowed her to be sensitive to the needs of others. She has a heart for God's people. She has endured harsh tests and trials as a young Christian and is now able to use her testimony of triumph to break the chains and strongholds from around the necks of others. As a first lady, she would often be led to fast, pray, and shut in with the saints all night at the altar. Her obedience has resulted in many being delivered, set free, and made whole. For many years she held Spiritual Warfare Classes. She has been anointed by God to teach the saints how to use the Word as their weapon, identify the enemy and his tactic, and annihilate his plan. She would later start and become the CEO of "Joyce Ruth Haddon Ministries" a ministry dedicated to helping hurting people. Through the partners of this ministry, she has been able to bless families with cars, bill money, food, furniture, clothes, and so much more.

Joyce Ruth Haddon Ministries held yearly events catered around helping the hurting. Themes include "Be made whole," which addressed the brokenness of the woman, "R.E.D" (Restoring Everything Damages), and "Open Heaven," which helped individuals embrace the favor and overflow of God. Dr. Haddon is an Author.

Her books include "Chain Breaker," the book and journal, "New Season New Battle," "Priceless Woman," and a Spiritual Warfare Journal. The anointing of Dr. Joyce Haddon has allotted her to minister not only in the United States but in Africa, Trinidad, Hong Kong, Tai Pei, The Netherlands, Italy, Amsterdam, and The Philippines, which have resulted in healing, signs, and wonders in her ministry. There are testimonies of people being healed from cancer, deformities of the body, young women being delivered from ungodly relationships, depression, and suicide, blood issues drying up in the middle of service, and lumps disappearing during the service.

The same young woman that many declared would be found dead in an alley because of her lifestyle has been saved for over 55 years. She pastored along with her husband for over 48 years in Inkster and in Detroit, Michigan. She is the National Woman's Supervisor for the Pentecostal Outpour International Fellowship of Churches. Dr. Haddon lives in Michigan with her husband. She has five gifted children (four of whom are International Artists) and over 20 grandchildren. Dr. Haddon has many spiritual sons and daughters and is known all over the world as a Prophetess, Author, Actress, Motivator, Psalmist, Preacher, and Teacher.

Prioritizing My Battles
By Dr. Jacquie Hadnot

What does it mean to prioritize? To prioritize means to assign a higher level of importance, value, or attention to one task, goal, or activity over others. It involves making deliberate choices and decisions about allocating your time, resources, and energy based on what is most significant, urgent, or valuable.

When you prioritize, you determine the order in which tasks or goals should be addressed, considering factors such as deadlines, impact, relevance, and personal or organizational objectives. Prioritizing helps you focus on what matters most, increase productivity, manage time effectively, and achieve desired outcomes.

Prioritization often involves evaluating the relative importance and urgency of different tasks or goals and making informed decisions about allocating your efforts accordingly. It requires assessing the potential consequences of other choices and deciding which actions will have the most significant impact or contribute most to your objectives.

In essence, prioritizing involves consciously determining what needs to be done first, what can be postponed or delegated, and what can be omitted altogether, allowing you to make the most efficient and effective use of your resources and efforts. I learned a long time ago to pick my battles and be strategic. Taking on unnecessary battles always left me mentally, physically, and emotionally drained.

WHAT DOES IT MEAN TO PRIORITIZE MY BATTLES

To "*prioritize your battles*" means to choose which conflicts or challenges are worth your time, attention, and energy. It involves selecting the battles or disagreements that are most important, significant, or meaningful to you while letting go of or not engaging in those that are less significant or not worth your effort. If you don't choose your battles, they might choose you, and often, the unprioritized battles will leave you weak and war-weary.

Prioritizing your battles is about recognizing that you cannot fight every battle or address every conflict that comes your way. It is an acknowledgment that your time and energy are limited resources, and you need to use them wisely. Remember, some battles aren't battles; they are distractions disguised as skirmishes.

By prioritizing your battles, you focus your efforts on the issues that align with your values, goals, principles, or those that significantly impact your well-being or the well-being of others. It helps you avoid unnecessary conflicts or getting caught up in trivial disagreements that distract you from what truly matters.

Prioritizing your battles also means considering the potential consequences of conflict. You must assess whether the issue is worth the potential adverse outcomes, such as damaged relationships, increased stress, or wasted resources. It requires evaluating the long-term benefits and weighing them against the potential costs.

Prioritizing your battles involves carefully choosing which conflicts to engage in and which to let go of, focusing your efforts on the most important and impactful issues, and being mindful of the potential consequences of your choices.

WHAT DOES IT MEAN TO FIGHT WITH CLARITY

To "***fight with clarity***" means to engage in battles or conflicts with a clear understanding of your purpose, goals, and values. It involves having a focused and well-defined perspective on the battle, enabling you to make informed decisions, communicate effectively, and take decisive action.

When you fight with clarity, you have a clear vision of what you are fighting for and why it matters. You can articulate your intentions, objectives, and desired outcomes. This clarity of purpose provides a solid foundation and helps you stay focused, motivated, and determined in the face of challenges.

Fighting with clarity also involves understanding the broader context and implications of the battle. It means considering the potential consequences of your actions and evaluating the short-term and long-term impact. This awareness allows you to make strategic choices and prioritize battles that align with your values and have a meaningful impact.

Fighting with clarity involves effective communication. It means expressing your ideas, concerns, and goals clearly and concisely, ensuring that others understand your perspective. Clarity in communication helps to avoid misunderstandings, build stronger relationships, and garner support for your cause.

Fighting with clarity requires self-awareness and emotional intelligence. It means understanding your strengths, weaknesses, and triggers, as well as being aware of the emotions and motivations of others. This awareness allows you to navigate conflicts with empathy and resilience, making sound decisions even in the midst of intense battles.

Overall, fighting with clarity means clearly understanding your purpose, goals, values, and the broader context of the battle. It involves effective communication, self-awareness, and strategic decision-making. By fighting with clarity, you are better equipped to navigate conflicts, pursue meaningful objectives, and make a positive impact.

Having clarity when engaging in a battle is important for several reasons:

- **Focus and direction**: Clarity provides you with a clear focus and direction in the midst of a battle. It helps you understand what you are fighting for and why it matters, allowing you to channel your energy and efforts towards the most important aspects of the battle. Without clarity, you may become easily distracted or lose sight of your objectives, hindering your effectiveness.
  - Ephesians 6:12 (NIV): "*For our struggle is not against flesh and blood, but against the rulers, against the authorities, against the powers of this dark world and against the spiritual forces of evil in the heavenly realms.*" This verse reminds us that our battles are not merely physical or against other people, but they have a spiritual dimension.

- **Strategic decision-making**: Clarity enables you to make strategic decisions during a battle. When you clearly understand your goals and values, you can assess different options, evaluate potential risks and benefits, and choose the most effective course of action. Clarity helps you prioritize battles, allocate resources wisely, and make informed decisions that align with your desired outcomes.

- Proverbs 16:3 (NIV): "*Commit to the LORD whatever you do, and he will establish your plans.*" By committing our battles and priorities to the Lord, we acknowledge His sovereignty and seek His guidance in our decision-making. Prioritizing battles with God's wisdom and guidance leads to greater success.

- **Effective communication**: Clarity facilitates effective communication with others involved in the battle. When you clearly understand your purpose and goals, you can articulate your ideas, concerns, and intentions more effectively. Clear communication helps build understanding, fosters collaboration, and increases the likelihood of finding common ground or resolving conflicts amicably.

- **Resilience and perseverance**: Clarity provides a sense of purpose and motivation, even in the face of adversity. Having a clear vision of what you are fighting for can help you stay resilient, persevere through challenges, and overcome obstacles. Clarity is a source of strength and determination, helping you stay focused and committed to your cause.

- **Alignment with values**: Clarity ensures that your battles are aligned with your values and principles. It helps you assess whether the battle is worth fighting, considering the ethical, moral, and personal implications. Clarity allows you to engage in meaningful battles that align with who you are, promoting a sense of integrity and authenticity in your actions.

- **Reduced stress and uncertainty**: When you have clarity about your objectives, strategies, and priorities, it reduces stress and uncertainty. Clarity provides a sense of confidence and peace of mind, as you have a clear roadmap to follow. It helps you navigate the battle with greater calmness and assurance.

Clarity in a battle is crucial for focus, decision-making, communication, resilience, values alignment, and reducing stress. It empowers you to make purposeful choices, stay on track, and increase your chances of achieving positive outcomes.

STRATEGIES ON HOW TO PRIORITIZE YOUR BATTLES

Here are some strategies to help you prioritize your battles effectively:

- **Take the battle to God in Prayer:** Your greatest strategy will be birthed in prayer. 2 Chronicles 20:15 (NIV): *"He said: 'Listen, King Jehoshaphat and all who live in Judah and Jerusalem! The LORD says this: Do not be afraid or discouraged because of this vast army. For the battle is not yours, but God's.'"* In this passage, King Jehoshaphat is assured by God that the battle belongs to the Lord, emphasizing the importance of relying on God's strength in times of conflict.

- **Define your goals:** Identify your overarching goals and objectives. This will help you align your battles with what truly matters to you and avoid wasting time on trivial matters.

Proverbs 21:5 (NIV): "The plans of the diligent lead to profit as surely as haste leads to poverty." This verse emphasizes the importance of careful planning and diligent decision-making. Prioritizing battles requires thoughtful consideration and wise planning to ensure our efforts yield positive outcomes.

- **Assess the significance:** Evaluate each battle's importance and potential impact. Consider how it aligns with your values, long-term aspirations, and the well-being of yourself and others. Focus on battles that have a meaningful and positive outcome.

- **Consider urgency**: Determine the urgency of each battle by evaluating deadlines, time-sensitive factors, and immediate consequences. Addressing time-sensitive battles first can help prevent escalation or further complications.

- **Weigh the consequences**: Assess the potential positive and negative consequences of engaging in a particular battle. Consider the potential benefits, risks, and potential impact on relationships. This evaluation will help you decide which battles are worth pursuing and which to let go of.

- **Prioritize based on resources:** Evaluate the resources required for each battle, including time, energy, and other assets. Be realistic about your capacity to engage in multiple battles simultaneously. Prioritize battles within your means, and don't spread yourself too thin.

- **Seek wise counsel**: Consult trusted individuals who can provide valuable insights and perspectives on your battles. Their input can help you gain clarity and make more informed decisions about which battles to prioritize.

- **Let go of unnecessary battles**: Recognize that not every battle is worth fighting. Learn to discern between battles that contribute to your growth and well-being and those that are draining or distracting. Practice letting go and focus your energy on battles that truly matter.

- **Practice self-care:** Prioritize self-care to ensure you have the energy, resilience, and clarity to engage in battles effectively. Taking care of your physical, emotional, and mental well-being will enable you to approach battles with a clear and focused mindset.

- **Consider long-term impact**: Look beyond immediate outcomes and the long-term effects of engaging in a particular battle. Some battles may have a lasting impact on your life or the lives of others, while others may be temporary or inconsequential in the grand scheme of things.

- **Align with your strengths**: Prioritize battles that leverage your expertise. By focusing on areas where you have a natural advantage or knowledge, you can maximize your effectiveness and increase your chances of success. Psalm 18:39 (NIV): "*You armed me with strength for battle; you humbled my adversaries before me.*"

- **Evaluate opportunity costs**: Recognize that when you engage in one battle, you may need to sacrifice or postpone others. Assess the opportunity costs of each battle and determine if the potential benefits outweigh what you might be giving up.

- **Break it down like a shotgun**: If you face multiple complex battles, break them down into smaller, manageable tasks or sub-battles. Prioritize the key steps or components that will have the most significant impact and tackle them individually.

- **Learn from past experiences:** Reflect on past battles and the lessons learned. Consider what worked well and what didn't. Apply these insights to make more informed decisions about prioritizing future battles and avoiding unnecessary conflicts.

- **Maintain flexibility**: Be open to adjusting your priorities as circumstances change. New information or developments may require you to reassess the importance or order of your battles. Stay adaptable and willing to make adjustments when necessary.

- **Trust your instincts:** Trust your intuition and inner guidance when prioritizing battles. Pay attention to your instincts and gut feelings. They can often provide valuable insights and help you make decisions aligned with your priorities.

Remember, prioritizing battles is an ongoing process that may require regular reassessment and adjustment. Priorities can shift as circumstances change, so remain adaptable and willing to reprioritize when needed. Using these strategies, you can navigate your battles more effectively and focus on what truly matters to you. Joshua 1:9 (NIV): *"Have I not commanded you? Be strong and courageous. Do not be afraid; do not be discouraged, for the LORD your God will be with you wherever you go."*

SCRIPTURES ON PRIORITIZING MY BATTLES

Matthew 6:33 (NIV): "*But seek first his kingdom and his righteousness, and all these things will be given to you as well.*" This verse reminds us to prioritize seeking God's kingdom and righteousness. By aligning our battles with God's will and purposes, we can find clarity in prioritizing what truly matters.

Psalm 90:12 (NIV): "*Teach us to number our days, that we may gain a heart of wisdom.*" This verse highlights the significance of recognizing the preciousness of our time. Prioritizing battles requires wisdom in understanding that our time and energy are limited, and we must use them wisely for the things that truly matter.

Ecclesiastes 3:1 (NIV): "*There is a time for everything and a season for every activity under the heavens.*" This passage reminds us that there is a proper time and season for different activities and battles. Prioritizing battles involves discerning the appropriate timing and focusing on the most relevant and timely battles in our lives.

Philippians 4:8 (NIV): "*Finally, brothers and sisters, whatever is true, whatever is noble, whatever is right, whatever is pure, whatever is lovely, whatever is admirable—if anything is excellent or praiseworthy—think about such things.*" This verse encourages us to focus on the things that are true, noble, and worthy of praise. When prioritizing battles, we can consider which battles align with these qualities and contribute to positive outcomes.

Proverbs 24:27 (NIV): "*Put your outdoor work in order and get your fields ready; after that, build your house.*" This verse emphasizes the importance of proper order and sequence. Prioritizing battles involves putting essential tasks in order, and addressing foundational or necessary matters before moving on to secondary battles.

Psalm 37:5 (NIV): "*Commit your way to the LORD; trust in him, and he will do this.*" This verse encourages us to trust the Lord and commit our battles to Him. When we prioritize our battles, relying on God's guidance and strength, we can confidently believe He will work on our behalf.

James 3:17 (NIV): *"But the wisdom that comes from heaven is first pure; then peace-loving, considerate, submissive, full of mercy and good fruit, impartial and sincere."* This verse describes heavenly wisdom and its characteristics. When prioritizing battles, we can seek to align ourselves with these qualities, choosing battles that promote peace, considerate actions, mercy, and good fruit.

Psalm 46:10 (NIV*): "He says, 'Be still, and know that I am God; I will be exalted among the nations, I will be exalted in the earth.'"* This verse reminds us to be still and trust in God's sovereignty. When prioritizing battles, we must take moments of stillness and seek God's guidance, allowing Him to lead us and exalt Himself in our battles.

Dr. Jacquie Hadnot

Genuine leadership is found among those audacious enough to signal the importance of others to the rest of the world. The compassionate professional Dr. Jacquie Hadnot is trailblazing a path where philanthropy meets world-class ingenuity.

Dr. Jacquie is an International best-selling author, cleric, entrepreneurial enthusiast, and Founder of Mallie Boushaye Essentials and Purpose Life Coaching. No stranger to establishing anomalous conglomerates, Dr. Hadnot has enjoyed the flexibility of sustaining a six-figure manufacturing and retail business without compromising the mandate of her life's core intendment: the will to inspire, empower, and implore people. Reputed for her uncanny ability to shift perspectives, enthuse purpose, and invoke change in diverse clientele, Jacquie remains a highly sought-after proponent in business, ministry, and social purlieus.

Dr. Jacquie combines unyielding excellence with sincere regard for education, achievement, and community involvement. She holds a Ph.D. in Pastoral Theology, an MA in Leadership, a BA in Theology, and a degree in Accounting. In addition to her propensity for educational understanding, she has also attained life, business, and cancer care coaching certifications. Her contributions in vocation, workshop facilitation, and ministerial advancements are awe-inspiring, as she has managed to lead in sales and ethics and in creating quintessential forms of humanitarianism, including support groups and multi-dimensional outreach programs. Dr. Jacquie's serviceability has proven highly prolific, as she was the 2022 recipient of the Joe Biden Presidential Lifetime Achievement

Award, easily yielding her as one of the most effective leaders of our time.

    Whether coaching the masses, empowering entrepreneurs, or overseeing her television network, Dr. Jacquie displays no corroboration in slowing down. When she is not out leaving a lasting impression on the world, she is an asset to her local communal body and a loving member of her family and friendship circles.

I Can't Afford To Fight You Too!
By Dr. Deborah Allen

I can't afford to fight you too" stands as an integral cornerstone within this anthology, wielding a profound significance as it underscores the pivotal need for discernment in identifying the battles that truly warrant your engagement. Beyond its role as a clarion call for strategic prioritization, this phrase serves as a stark revelation that, in your journey, you may find yourself contending with adversaries you never fathomed would cross your path. You may be experiencing fighting at home or work as you strive to become the best version of yourself. I think this is not strange because it is expected. Even as a Woman of God and entrepreneur, I have experienced this. Nevertheless, remember not to let anyone put their foot on your neck. In this shifting and challenging world, we grapple with the pressing need to carefully discern and prioritize the battles we choose to engage in. Life, with its multifaceted complexities and relentless demands, presents a series of trials and tribulations. In this very context, the resounding and resolute declaration takes shape: "I can't afford to fight you too!" This phrase encapsulates the notion that as we ascend the ladder of personal growth and navigate the uncharted waters of our professional lives, we are invariably faced with various conflicts and adversities, each vying for our attention and energy.

Oh, warriors, let's hold our ground and be wise in our plans, lives, and movements! We must adopt a discerning approach when allocating our time and energy to our endeavors, for in prioritizing your battles, you gain a profound clarity that allows you to distinguish between those challenges and adversaries you actively confront and those that subtly assail you. In the midst of life's constant change and whirlwind of activity, where many elements vying for your attention and devotion, it is essential not to succumb to the allure of being distracted.

PRIORITIZING MY BATTLES

You can navigate the complexities of existence with an unwavering sense of purpose and determination by steadfastly focusing on your chosen battles and not allowing the tumultuous currents of simultaneous occurrences to divert your course. Be fierce at this moment and prepare yourself to be strategic to battle and ultimately build. Don't be discouraged; you must prioritize your battles and not sweat small things.

The weight of this declaration becomes increasingly pronounced when we consider the broader implications of our choices in this regard. It serves as an unmistakable reminder that, in a world teeming with challenges and opportunities alike, we must exercise a strategic approach to determine which battles are truly worth our investment of time, energy, and resources. Our capacity to succeed and thrive is fundamentally contingent on our ability to make these determinations wisely, ensuring that our efforts are channeled into endeavors that align with our values, goals, and dreams. We must harness our inner strength and resilience as we navigate these tumultuous waters. The battles we choose to confront often serve as crucibles in which our character is forged and our mettle tested. They symbolize our unwavering determination and unyielding commitment to personal and professional growth.

It is important to recognize that, along the path to self-improvement, we may encounter battles in the professional arena and within the confines of our own homes. This confluence of personal and professional struggles should not be viewed as a strange or isolated phenomenon; rather, it is a shared experience among individuals striving to realize their fullest potential. Even those who proudly identify as Women of God and entrepreneurs have traversed the arduous terrain of self-discovery and development, encountering their fair share of opposition and resistance. Through these challenges, we derive strength and resilience, forging a path toward our authentic selves.

Yet, amidst the voices and the turmoil of conflict, we must remain steadfast in our purpose. We cannot allow others to exert control or stifle the burgeoning voices within us. As we embark on the journey of self-expression and self-actualization, we may encounter individuals who seek to undermine our efforts, diminish our voices, and thwart our aspirations. In these moments, the refrain "I can't afford to fight you too!" reverberates most profoundly, reminding us of the critical need to preserve our focus and energies for pursuits that truly matter. Like a wellspring of vitality, our energy is a finite resource. To dissipate it in fruitless battles against those who seek to silence us is to squander our most precious asset. Instead, let us stand resolute in our convictions, unwavering determination, and unyielding in our pursuit of personal and professional excellence. By selectively and strategically choosing our battles, we ensure that our energy is channeled into endeavors that propel us forward, enabling us to grow, dream, and build the futures we envision for ourselves. In this deliberate and purposeful approach to life's challenges, we find the strength to survive and thrive.

- Strategic Battle Selection: In life's complexity, selecting the battles we engage in strategically is crucial. The phrase "I can't afford to fight you too!" emphasizes the

need to prioritize and invest our time and energy wisely.
- Resilience Through Adversity: Challenges and conflicts are not obstacles but opportunities for personal growth and resilience. They forge our character and test our determination, enabling us to become stronger and more resilient individuals.
- Striving for Excellence: By selectively and strategically choosing our battles, we ensure our energy is directed towards endeavors that align with our values and aspirations. This deliberate approach empowers us to survive and thrive in life's grand tapestry.

"I can't afford to fight you too" is an uplifting reminder for us not to be sidetracked by battles that don't align with our highest goals and aspirations. When I prioritize my battles, embracing the empowering truth behind "I can't afford to fight you, too!" declares my commitment to focus on endeavors that truly matter and elevate me to new heights of success and fulfillment.

ACKNOWLEDGMENTS

This tribute is dedicated in this time of necessity to every individual who has encountered the arduous journey of self-growth, self-reinvention, self-belief, and self-love. May these words serve as an enduring testament to the exceptional tenacity and fearless determination of those who courageously embrace their identity and faith. You may remain focused on your purpose and fight with strategy and clarity.

I sincerely love Lighthouse Apostolic Ministries of God Church, "The House of The Prophets." They have graciously allowed me to be their Pastor these last 24 years. It has been inspiring to serve with this body of believers. Jesus, I'm forever indebted to you. Unconditionally, I am your willing servant and a grateful prisoner of the Gospel!

Much love to my natural family, children, friends, clients, and all the saints for their love and support. Again, I say thank you.

"When walking in purpose, fiercely walk in divine authority."
Apostle Dr. Deborah Allen

Dr. Deborah Allen

Finding one's *inner voice* can be a liberating, awe-inspiring, and transformational experience. The dynamic professional Deborah Allen is fashioned to help the masses find their "fierce."

Deborah Allen is a 47X best-selling & 23X international best-selling author, speaker, certified life coach, cleric, and CEO and creative founder of "The Fierce System," a multifaceted liaison specialty centered around helping women find and develop their voice. Having been trained by world-renowned NSA motivational speaker Mr. Les Brown, Deborah understands the importance of strategy, development, and credible mentorship, traits she seamlessly translates to her growing clientele.

Deborah's mantra is simple: Her only goal is to motivate clients, helping them to create the life they were meant to live.

Refusing mediocrity on all fronts, Deborah has trailblazed a credible path for those she serves. She has served as Senior Pastor of Lighthouse Apostolic Ministries of God Church for the last 24 years and is the Executive Director of the nonprofit organization L.A.M. Ministries, Inc.

Deborah is a Certified Life Coach who matches servant leadership with an incredible respect for higher learning. She is a member of the National Speaker Association Speaker (NSA) and a Black Speakers Network (BSN) Speaker. Her conglomerate, The Fierce System, comprises many platforms, including Fierce TV, Radio, and blog and Fierce Voices of Destiny Program, where she mentors, develops, and creates strategic alignment between clients and their true life's calling. She is the Visionary and CEO of Igniting The Flame

Publishing, Visionary Coaching & Consulting Group LLC, and Deborah Allen Enterprise. Dr. Deborah graduated on October 29, 2022, with her Dr. of Philosophy and Christian Leadership from Cornerstone Christian University in Atlanta, GA.

Deborah proudly attests that women are at the heartbeat of all she does and that she desires to see them be strong and fierce, know that they can truly achieve their dreams, and walk in purpose. When she is not helping women come alive, rebuild, shift, and find themselves again, Deborah is a valued asset to her communal body and a loving member of her family and friendship circles.

Dr. Deborah Allen. Energizer. Organizer. Servant Leader

Contact Information:
Apostle Dr. Deborah Allen

www.deborahallenfierce.com
www.ignitingtheflamepublishing.com
Email: deborahallenfierce@gmail.com
Links:
Facebook: https://www.facebook.com/deborahallenfierce
Instagram: https://www.instagram.com/deborahallenfierce/
Twitter: https://twitter.com/deborahallenfie
YouTube: https://www.youtube.com/channel/UCTOf0igcAxlVaneH2ZOo_Zg
2nd Website: https://deborahallenspeaker.com/

Choose Your Battles Wisely: WWJD?
(What Would Jesus Do?)
By Featured Author, Dr. Pamela Henkel

I love my life, ALL of it. But it has not always been that way. It was not an accident or mere luck. It took perseverance, dedication, and, most importantly, choosing the right battles. I have seen many storms and learned that every storm must not be confronted head-on.

In my younger years, I was fiery, always ready to argue my point. My background in the debate team and my 15 years teaching debate had something to do with that! (LOL) But over the years, I have learned a profound truth: Most people do not wake up intending to offend or hurt you. Many times, they're oblivious to the pain they might cause. How often have we let ourselves get upset over perceived slights, losing our peace in the process?

> *"For God is not the author of confusion but of peace."* - 1 Corinthians 14:33

I vividly remember the season that completely changed my perspective on this. Our youngest son, born prematurely at 24 weeks, fought for his life in the NICU. I sat by his side daily, praying, believing, and dealing with many emotions. With five other children, a business, and a ministry to manage, my life was overwhelming. The stress started taking a toll on my health. Sleep eluded me, and my eating habits were far from ideal. My body began sending signals in the form of palpitations.

One particular day stands out. I arrived at the NICU with a grim prognosis from a doctor about our son's survival chances. At that moment, something within me snapped. I remember drawing a line in the sand and asking the doctor to leave the room. I declared that no one was to enter if they didn't have words of faith and love for our son. (Today, I am so glad I said those words.) As I held my baby close, my heart racing, feeling overwhelmed with all that was happening in my life, our nurse walked in, her concern evident. Through gentle tears, I whispered my frustrations. Her words of wisdom were a game-changer: "Pick and choose your battles, Pamela."

Could it be that simple? A visit to the cardiologist confirmed that my heart was healthy, but my spirit was weary. "You need to decompress," he advised.

How do I do that? I turned to God. I pleaded, "Holy Spirit, help me. Guide me to decompress." I felt His whisper, "I have been waiting for you to ask."

"Peace I leave with you; the peace I give to you. Not as the world gives do I give to you. Let not your hearts be troubled, neither let them be afraid."
- John 14:27

Embracing this newfound revelation, looking for a way to begin again... I became a yoga teacher. This introduced me to a new way to connect one-on-one with my Savior and find that Shalom Peace of God. Contrary to misconceptions, yoga becomes a conduit to quieten one's mind, hear God more clearly, and decompress when done with the right intent. With a combination of breathing exercises, stretching, and prayer, I found my sanctuary.

Every day, on my mat, I would surrender everything to Him. My focus would sharpen, and all that existed was Jesus and me. Peace started seeping into my life. Viewing others through Christ's eyes brought compassion, understanding, and patience. Situations that once flustered me were now met with spiritual authority and trust in God's plan. The daily practice of quoting scriptures about peace, joy, and God's protective armor became my mantra. As my thinking shifted, my beliefs, behaviors, and results transformed.

"Other people's opinion of you does not have to become your reality." - Les Brown.

Today, I am a testament to what choosing your battles can achieve. Our miracle son, who once fought for every breath, has thrived for 14 years. I remember watching him one day during a school event; it dawned on me—the palpitations had disappeared, replaced with pure, unadulterated peace. Tears flowed, but this time, they were tears of joy.

As we navigate life, battle options will be varied and numerous. However, the choice in each confrontation isn't just between engagement or retreat, but 'how will choosing this battle serve me or my purpose?' Below are some key ideas God has given to help me choose my battles.

The Subtle Power of Perception

Over the years, I have realized that perception dramatically influences our battles. Do we view the battle as a threat or a lesson?

It is not just about external conflicts; it's also about the internal narratives we weave. By changing our perspective, we can often transform a potential battle into a bridge of understanding.

WWJ- Perceive?

Emotional Energy and its Finite Nature

Every battle requires energy – emotional, mental, and sometimes physical. However, our emotional reservoir is not infinite. We have one bag of energy and must use it wisely. If we continually drain it by engaging in every skirmish that comes our way, we risk depleting our inner strength. There is a profound wisdom in discerning where to invest our bag of energy. By choosing battles carefully, we ensure that our fights are not just reactionary but purpose-driven.

WWJ- Do?

The Wisdom in Silence

I've found that silence can be a powerful weapon in my journey. Contrary to popular belief, choosing not to engage is not a sign of weakness but one of strength. There are situations where silence speaks volumes. It provides space for introspection and healing and, sometimes, lets the storm pass without causing havoc.

WWJ- Speak?

The Ripple Effect of Our Choices

Every battle engaged has repercussions, not just for us but for those around us. By choosing our battles wisely, we demonstrate the value of discernment. Our actions become a living testament, a wisdom that speaks louder than words.

WWJ- Choose?

Navigating Battles with Grace

While it is essential to choose our battles, it is equally important to approach them with grace when we decide to engage. It means engaging with integrity and respect. This approach does not just help in resolving conflicts but also ensures that bridges are still in the process.

The battles were many in my most challenging times, especially during those heart-wrenching days in the NICU. But the realization that I had a choice in how to respond was empowering. It was not about avoiding the battles but facing them with a heart filled with faith, hope, and love. And in this delicate dance between confrontation and compassion, I found a rhythm that kept me at peace.

WWJ- Decide?

The Armor of Discernment

This discernment is born from experience, wisdom, and faith. It enables us to see the immediate challenge and the broader perspective – And sometimes, this bird's eye view makes all the difference. It helps us differentiate between a fleeting storm and an imminent hurricane.

WWJ- Discern?

Embracing Vulnerability in Our Battles

In a culture that often equates vulnerability to weakness, it is essential to recognize its strengths. We realize that being vulnerable means we do not need to have all the answers. In this acceptance lies strength – the power to seek help, lean on a friend, or pause and take a breath.

During those tense moments in the NICU, vulnerability was not my enemy but my ally. It allowed me to seek comfort, express my fears, and, most importantly, remain authentic. By doing so, I was not just coping; I was healing.

WWJ- Do to seek comfort?

Interconnected Battles

Our battles are not just external; many are waged within. An inner battle not dealt with can lead to a full-blown war showing up in our bodies, just like I experienced with the palpitations. This understanding became real to me when I entered the world of yoga. My body changed through controlled breathing, deliberate stretches, and meditation/prayer. Not just how I looked but how I felt on the inside. My spiritual life grew exponentially as the times on the mat became a sanctuary between The Holy Spirit and myself.

WWJ- To find sanctuary

Re-defining Victory

In the grand scheme, winning is not always about fighting to win. Sometimes, victory is about growth, learning, and transformation. It is about recognizing that every scar and every wound has a story. Thus creating a higher awareness to choose one's battles.

Looking back, I realize that my most significant victories weren't the battles I won but the ones I chose to sidestep. Doing so, my body decompressed, I cherished my peace, retained my joy, and preserved relationships.

WWJ- Sidestep?

In the words of Les Brown, "Life has no limitations except the ones you make." We are not limiting ourselves but liberating our spirit by choosing our battles. Each decision is a testament to our wisdom, growth, and the depth of our journey with God.

In this tremendous life journey, we must decide what is worth our energy and what is not. Drawing strength from Proverbs 3:5-6, "Trust in the LORD with all your heart and lean not on your understanding; in all your ways submit to Him, and He will make your paths straight." As you navigate choosing battles, let God's wisdom guide you, ensuring every decision is not just a reaction but a response out of faith.

My dear friend, pick and choose your battles wisely. Let God be your defender. **Choose The Way Of Peace!**

"Choose your battles wisely. After all, life isn't measured by how many times you stand up to fight. It's not winning battles that make you happy, but how many times you turned away and chose to look in a better direction. Life is too short to spend it on warring. Fight only the most, most, most important ones, let the rest go." - C. JoyBell C.

Dr. Pamela Henkel

Individuals seasoned with generous charisma, compassion, and undeniable essence possess the ingenuity that shifts the world into its greatness. The spirited professional, Dr. Pamela Henkel, is stewarding these traits in unyielding measure. Dr. Pamela Henkel is an International Best-Selling Author, multifaceted compere, speaker, elite coach, CEO, and Founder of Purpose with Pamela and Pamela Henkel Ministries. Her multifaceted production and International radio conglomerate are fashioned to enthuse women, entrepreneurs, authors, and diverse professionals to take hold of their life's purpose.

Dr. Pamela Henkel's mission is to add value to as many lives as possible. She reminds them they are here purposefully with a Purpose by Design, not by default. Partnering her passions with sincere regard for higher learning, community, and achievement, Dr. Pamela Henkel's career remains a reflection of creative grace, captivating the hearts and minds of many.

She holds a doctorate in Philosophy, Christian Leadership, and Business and is on the Board of Regents for Cornerstone University.

Living life as one dedicated to the service of people, Dr. Henkel has maintained a nonpareil presence in the modern business world. As the creative founder of The Prestigious Purpose Awards, The Pamela Show, and more, she extends her podcast, International radio, and social platforms to promote the voices of many globally. Her propensity for success in her field has led her to award-winning achievements, such as the nomination as one of the Top 50 Women of Business, an elite membership of the Power Voice, and personal mentorship from the world-renowned speaker and mentor Les Brown. Dr. Henkel also received the Unsung Hero Award for helping people get the education they desire and deserve. Dr. Henkel's expertise has led to her positions as Elite Head Coach at the Million in You Academy and as an International Speaker and minister. She's also featured in the docudrama Think And Grow Rich Moms Rising, inspiring and empowering women to reach their full potential.

Dr. Pamela Henkel calls Minnesota home, where she enjoys spending time with her family and family pets. She cherishes the moments she gets to share with her loved ones. As well as always encouraging people to be the salt and the light everywhere they go.

Dr. Pamela Henkel. Leader. Energizer. Philanthropist.
www.purposewithpamela.com
https://linktr.ee/Purposewithpamela

Don't Come For Me; I Didn't Send For You
By Dr. Cindy Betts

Yes, battle ready to confront and conquer. So, don't let this beautiful smile, sensual and self-effacing personality in this little person's body deceive you because the value of my oil can't be compromised.

I am not a spiritual pushover, nor am I a spiritual punk. God brought me through too much to see if he could trust me with it. Do you think I have time to entertain my adversaries' distractions, disruptions, and disturbances targeting my potential, purpose, or my peace to battle with my brothers' and sisters' foolery too? Not today, and tomorrow doesn't look too good either!

FYI, Cushites & 20th Century Israelites! Unapologetically, I prioritize my battles, so I don't have time to fight with you church folks, too! Believe that, believers! Canton Jones sings it best for me, "I'm Just Trying to Stay Saved! Jesus knows that's my battle every second in the minute of the hour within a day for this kingdom, kid. If I could sing professionally, I would always use my praise power to be like the wind and blow anything disrupting my peace into the abyss. But until then, I'll make a joyful noise and do the same! LOL

Transparent moment: Why I'm sharing my story is to shift your thinking regarding issues, situations, problems, trials, and tribulations that are mine and possibly yours too. I have been truly tested and must endure my storms. Yes, I can, and so can you, but you must trust the same God as I do! You must use the same power as I **PRAY (peace restoration is yours).** Say it to you see it; Call it till it comes! Put a word, then praise on it!

Beginning with Covid 19, I caught it twice while in Jamaica and had to leave before the new Jan 26th, 2019. the testing mandate for reentry into the US passed.

I would've been quarantined in Jamaica for eleven more days, but I wouldn't be free or on vacation. I also filed for bankruptcy for one of my tax service businesses that year, which continued to 2020.

2021: Family deaths, separation, job losses, so I became the cash cow. ATM for my children/grandchildren (automatically tell mommy). This kept going until the very end of the year.

2022: My Stripping- Covid (again); Divorce (filed two days before my birthday) Financial (loss stock/investments; Duress (peace disrupted).

I heard the HS tell me and give me the detailed instructions outlined in my journal below! He said, "Don't do NEW the same OLE way in 2022! God, "Where are you taking me? I'm just gonna tell you, "Yes!"

✓ <u>Don't DO NEW the same Ole Way.</u>

Definition of DO: VERB
1. Perform (an action, the precise nature of which is often unspecified).
2. Achieve or complete.
3. Act or behave in a specified way.

Definition of NEW: ADJECTIVE
1. Not existing before; made, introduced, or discovered recently or now for the first time.
2. Already existing but seen, experienced, or acquired recently or now for the first time.

3. Just beginning or beginning anew and regarded as better than what went before.

✓ <u>Name (3) DO things that are priorities and passions for you?</u> (2nd Instruction)

<u>God says throughout HIS word:</u> **Do** not fear, **Do** not be worried, **Do** not lie, **Do** not judge others, **Do** not be perceived, **Do** not be afraid, **Do** not turn to the proud, **Do** unto others as you would like unto you. This part! So why **Do** I have to fight with you? **Do** not come for me because I didn't send for you!
  ✓ <u>DO IT THIS WAY! (3rd Instruction)</u>
  1. <u>Ecclesiastes 9:10 (MSG) -Excellence</u>
  2. <u>Romans 12:1-2(MSG) -Dream and place your life before God.</u>

12 $^{1-2}$ So here's what I want you to do, God helping you: Take your everyday, ordinary life—your sleeping, eating, going to work, and walking around life—and place it before God as an offering. Embracing what God does for you is the best thing you can do for him. Don't become so well-adjusted to your culture that you fit into it without thinking. Instead, fix your attention on God. You'll be changed from the inside out. Readily recognize

what he wants from you and quickly respond to it. Unlike the culture around you, always dragging you down to its level of immaturity, God brings the best out of you and develops well-formed maturity in you.

   3. <u>1 Corinthians 10:31-33 (MSG) – Glory to God!</u>

So, what (3) things are you going to do NEW?

2 Corinthians 5:17 17 Therefore, if anyone is in Christ, the new creation has come: The old has gone, the new is here! Proverbs 1:5 5 Let the wise listen and add to their learning, and let the discerning get guidance. Therefore, follow these instructions to do new things!

   ✓ <u>Trying NEW things this way: (4th Instruction)</u>
   1. <u>Job 12:12 (MSG)</u> -Wisdom
   2. <u>Ecclesiastes 11:6(MSG)</u> -Sow Seed (time, talents & time)
   3. <u>2 Timothy 1:7 (MSG) -Fearless & Faithful</u>

DARE (Deny Adversary Risk Everything in Faith) requires bravery, the challenge to prove courage to **DREAM** (DoIt RightNow Experience All Master's Promises) visions, aspirations, ambitions, and great desires! Dream Big and Believe Bigger!

4. <u>Galatians 6:3,4(MSG) & Ephesians 6:4-5(MSG)</u> -Self Analytical

Although, after I followed these instructions, I left baggage and felt a transparent breakthrough through self-analysis. Self-analysis can also be called **introspection, self-contemplation, self-examination, and self-concept.** The X-ray in the DETOX must be consistent in your life. Oh, but that's not it!

> The **SACHET** also came in 2022! (sarcasm, abuse, criticism, hypocrisy, embarrassment, trials & tribulations.) I was a walking time bomb raising Tsunami hell. LAWD, pass this cup from ME! My aura had changed. I didn't smell fearfully and wonderfully made anymore. I smelt like a combination of musty and yesterday's repented sweat. I was so delusional, frustrated, and weary. I wept and cried out so loud I would constantly have a headache! I felt the heaviness and knew I was oppressed and under duress. **BUT** (better understand this) God!

HE heard my cry and told me to **SOAR** in 2023!

PRIORITIZING MY BATTLES

Stay
Out of the way
Allow Abba to
Restore & Rebuild You!

I said **YES** (yield everything for salvation)! And the adversary turned up the heat of **HELL** (havoc encumbering lethal limitations)!

The HELL In 2023:
- ✓ Jan-GA-No health insurance- Xhusband removes-$Cash for all treatment.
- ✓ Feb-GA-Judgement against business & then the ministry. Legal Malpractice
- ✓ Mar-GA- Loose wallet in Kroger parking lot/ NC Speeding Ticket from JOY retreat 2023.
- ✓ April- FL-Hospital-right hand surgery from a freak accident.
- ✓ May- LA- celebrated birthday alone.
- ✓ June- TN-Destiny's accident. Loss car
- ✓ July- INT-Soul Tie Purge
- ✓ Aug- GA- Final Divorce Decree -after 16 months
- ✓ Sept ~ Ghana~ Accra* -Volunteers bailed out
- ✓ Oct~ GA- Few Toys 4 Tots volunteers.

- ✓ Nov~ WI-St. Croix – Overbooked events
- ✓ Dec~ GA – Praying for **MORE** Party (manifested overflow restored expediently).

I must keep the enemy in the book! Philippians 4: 1-19. Whenever the enemy speaks to me, I have something to say. I don't give him what I think; I give him what God said. We can't use the temporal/carnal principalities on the eternal/spiritual standards. The fiery darts vs rubber knife. Lol Facts: The enemy/adversary sows seeds of havoc and confusion and will reap a harvest! We must speak life from our mouths and replace a carnal thought with an eternal thought. We are not a punching bag for the enemy/adversary. Nor are we the landing place for spiritual leeches.

My wilderness experience is my proven warfare ground. I didn't and couldn't rush the battle because it's being proven! Although my prayer life is on trial, God will take a trial and prove it. Hallelujah! Romans 8:37- I'm more than a Conqueror! Overcomers go through to grow through. So, please don't come for me because I didn't send for you! We all have glory from our story, so don't hate on mine!

PRIORITIZING MY BATTLES

Where are my **SWAT** Sisters or Brother?
Soldiers
With
A
Testimony!
The **SWAT**hood learns a method of defense called
The **SWATTER** tactic!
A SWATTER moves strategically.
Start
Wisking
Away
Things
That
Establish
Ramification

    Don't prey on me; Pray with me, and I with you. People would've brought me out to get me caught up in something else if I weren't careful. Don't let dilemma folks like you out either, and don't get so preoccupied with the situation to allow it to take over. LAWD, I ain't got time to fight church folk and them believers too! So, don't come for me, I didn't send for you! I truly prioritize my battle using a strategy that sets a standard for the enemy.

A Strategist in war is responsible for creating and making it happen—set goals, then the how actions, the materials, the process, then the execution. Strategies come from the word of God! His Jeremiah 29:11. I can just use my holy ghost's imagination if God were to tell us His will for Us. SMH, we would mess it up before it happens by making our own decisions. This only works best when your spiritual and natural abilities are working harmoniously.

- Note to self: When you try to get a breakthrough from **OWN** (Operate while nonaligned) strength,

stay extremely close and connected to God to get your strategy. God is committed to fulfilling HIS purpose in you, so I am committed to him to my kingdom assignment and all the challenges it brings.

Ephesians chapter one says, "Good things God spoke over me." The word remains until it enters my life, and my faith latches and links up with my gift. The power is in our words. We can't be blessed and bound. We can remind God of his promises for our lives. My protection is in my obedience because God will use my trouble to birth prosperity in my purpose.

SWAT members have K-9 attacks within their spiritual circle, so they must learn about the types of dogs to apply the **SWATTER** training move.
- ➢ Three (3) Types of Dogs in Ministry:
- ✓ <u>Wild Dog</u>:
- False people (don't have your best interest).
- They keep you praying to keep them away.
- Look tame until they bite you.
- ✓ <u>Wolf Dog</u>:
- False prophets – John 10: 11-15
- Come in packs- Ware you down and out.
- Meditate- Study and show thyself approved.
- ✓ <u>Hyenna Dog</u>:
- False Promises
- Distraction- False hope
- Weary worry wart worshipers.

Understand your **SWAT** brother or sister are carnal beings that fall short of the glory of God, so what makes one think you nor I are exceptions to this blatant statement of God? Some of these dogs have these leadership traits and initiate a false bite attack that will inflict deep pain and cause you to bleed and bruise so badly that you will need immediate first responder care.

Christian, Sir or Ma'am, I choose not to have you attack and bite me by any means. Not by incident, accident, or oops, my mistake! I am going through enough fighting with myself, myself, and I to add you to the equation. I've just shared my five straight years of ceaseless storms that God has stretched, broken, stripped, and tested me through. I can't and won't fight you and your battles too.

Let me drop this last Nataph nugget: **GET NEW NOW**!
Go after
Everything
The enemy stole.
No weapon formed against you prospers.
Everything has a time **BUT.**
Walk by faith!
Nothing
Overcomes
Warriors

PRIORITIZING MY BATTLES

LAWD, I ain't got time to fight church folk and them believers too! So, don't come for me, I didn't send for you! I can only please one person a day, and today isn't your day, and tomorrow ain't looking good either! The only person I am trying to please is God. I've finally been delivered from people and learned to live life in time as a wise person, not a fool. In other words, I am not living or moving by emotions or feelings but strategically by putting a word on it! We (U N I T Y are a unity- one body in Christ) Iron sharpening iron, servants serving together in the kingdom for his glory. Lawd, I ain't got time to fight the adversary and these believing church folk, too. Y'all read my story, so why hate on mine or anyone else's glory? You didn't contribute to the success and weren't there in the fall. The fact of the matter is I carried and covered you even when you didn't contribute! I truly am stronger than what you give me credit for, yet I still love you with the love of Christ, and there's nothing you can do about it!

I beseech you, my **SWAT** warrior brother or sister, reading this part right now; let's all get along and live prosperous, purposefully growing empires together for God's glory before the Parousia! Let's be a part of the solution, not the problem, to tell a dying world about a living Christ.

Let's stop being Spiritual K-9s attacking one another and devour and defeat the enemy at his trajectory to steal, kill, and destroy the kingdom of God and the body of Christ.   I just don't have time to fight the adversary, and you too! Don't come for me because I didn't send for you!

This chapter is from Dr. Cindy Betts' book,
"I AM Purpose- Who's I AM is GREATER than Who I AM."

Dr. Cindy Betts

Dr. Cindy Betts, formerly Bailey, is a born-again BELIEVER of Jesus Christ, BOLD about KINGDOM business, and a FEARLESS Prayer Warrior and intercessor for God's People—a native of Port-of-Spain, Trinidad, with Cuban and AA descent.

She's a King's Kid, a Queen, a Mother, a Grandmother, a Great-grandmother, an International Evangelist, a Teacher, a Certified Purpose Life Coach, Wealth Coach, (I AM Purpose Fragrance Collection, NVisionU, Purpose It's About Purpose Show-IHeart Radio -WDRB Media Station,

Author, Motivational & Leadership Speaker); Law Enforcement Counselor, So. Fulton County Annex Chaplin, Global Motivational BOSS Entrepreneur, Lecturer, Director of Operations, Financial Specialist, Certified Tax Preparer (IRS), Ordained Minister, K I N International Ministry Inc. Founder, Member of the Board (multiple organizations) & Former Bristol Hospice Chaplin.

Dr. Cindy holds an AAS in Accounting and Banking Operations, BBA with a Major in Finance, MA in Psychology -Family Counseling, MDiv- in Christian Counseling, and DMin- in Christian Counseling.

Dr. Cindy was awarded the "Western NY Humanity Award," & "Community Outreach Achiever 2000-2003" award, The Presidential Lifetime Achievement Award 2016, and many rewards not listed but found on the website. www.kininternationalministry.org

Dr. Cindy owns an AirBNB in Georgia, which will soon be built in Ghana Accra.

Dr Cindy is the surviving founder and Sister of the Freedom House Foundation in Ghana, Accra, for orphans (150) and widows (35). She has traveled to 23 countries and 40 states, consulting

& coaching wealth to build empires. Her greater will be her later with 172 countries & 12 cities more to travel!

Her Purpose: A Philanthropic 'Ambassador for Christ' as she lives her favorite scripture: Matthew 6:33Amplified Bible (AMP) 33 But first and most importantly seek (aim at, strive after) His kingdom and His righteousness [His way of doing and being right—the attitude and character of God], and all these things will be given to you also.

Love and hugs, Kingdom Kings & Queens! Have a great day on Purpose!

The Battle Of The Mind
By Dr. Phyllis Fuller

The mind is continually bombarded with many frequently opposing and contradictory notions. The mind is as vast and intricate as the universe, with billions of information moving through it, much like the countless stars. Studies have suggested a person has more than 6,000 thoughts per day. The battle of the mind is the mental struggle between these opposing ideas. The deliberations about which ideas to accept and focus on can be challenging. What enters the mind can enter the heart. If negative and unfruitful thoughts enter the heart and are not properly disregarded and abolished, they will be expressed in our lives and actions. Proverbs 4:23 encourages watching over your heart with all diligence because the springs of life flow from it.

In principle, keep your heart with all diligence, for out of it are the issues and treasures of life. The mental conflict over our decisions in every circumstance can be conquered by receiving and applying the Holy Scriptures. If we choose to do so, we can decide to make wise choices and reap the benefits of good actions. Romans 12:2 in the Voice Translation of the Holy Scriptures states, "Do not allow this world to mold you in its own image. Instead, be transformed from the inside out by renewing your mind. As a result, you will be able to discern what God wills and whatever God finds good, pleasing, and complete". The battle of the mind can be conquered. Four principles addressed in this writing are focusing on your thoughts, protecting your mind, overcoming distractions, and defying the negative opinions of others.

FOCUS TO FINISH

Knowing your core principles helps you respond in everyday situations and make important decisions. Setting meaningful priorities and developing a personal philosophy (both) depends on clearly understanding your values.

- Make a list of your values to get started.

- Decide on the three to five most important things to you.

The priorities you pursue must align with your core values if you want to have a feeling of purpose and accomplishment. To do that, you must evaluate your values and choose how to implement them. Establishing links between your values and your goals is required. Hopefully, your focus will be on the activities or interests that can help you express yourself and live in divine purpose and fulfillment. Be persistent and persevere. God has a good plan for your life. He has given you talents and abilities according to His plans and purposes.

Most meaningful advances demand that you labor regularly over a long period. Choose the everyday habits that will aid your success and give them top attention. Small actions repeated often are the first steps toward achieving major goals.

When a daily habit is carried out, the brain releases dopamine. Since it makes us happy and motivated, dopamine is sometimes called the "feel-good" neurotransmitter. Your brain will want you to repeat the connected behavior when it receives a rewarding boost from this neurotransmitter. These recurrent behaviors also result in significant changes over time. Through good times and bad, commitment is a circle of events that never ends. The Bible teaches in Proverbs 4:25, "Let your eyes look directly ahead and let your gaze be fixed straight in front of you." Even when nothing goes well, don't give up. Long-term consistency with your priorities and objectives requires effort and focus, so ensure you take all reasonable steps to feel encouraged and supported. Focus on finishing. Protecting your mind will also help you win the battle of your mind.

PROTECT YOUR MIND

We tend to assume that an idea must be true because it comes from within ourselves. But these ideas are sometimes not always true just because you think it is. I have witnessed the effects of mental illness. We constantly encounter incorrect notions because the world constantly feeds us false information. Of course, a defeated Satan, the evil one, sends fiery arrows to our minds to destroy our faith in God and His plan and purposes. However, our conqueror, Jesus Christ, gave us the winning solution. He provided armor to protect our whole being so that our whole spirit, soul, and body can be preserved blameless at the coming of our Lord Jesus Christ. The helmet of salvation to protect the mind is part of the armor of God. Ephesians 6:14-17: "Stand therefore, having your loins girt about with truth, and having on the breastplate of righteousness; And your feet shod with the preparation of the gospel of peace. Taking the shield of faith, wherewith ye shall be able to quench all the fiery darts of the wicked. And take the helmet of salvation and the sword of the Spirit, which is the word of God.

The word of God is protection for the mind. Romans 12:2 teaches, "And be not conformed to this world: but be ye transformed by the renewing of your mind, that ye may prove what is that good, and acceptable, and perfect, will of God." God's ways and thoughts are higher than yours. Protect your mind with the word of God. In so doing, your faith in God will be increased. You will win the battle of the mind. Consistently advancing in the things of God will require you to overcome distractions.

OVERCOME DISTRACTION

Oxford Languages Dictionary describes distraction as preventing someone from giving full attention to something else and extreme agitation of the mind or emotions. Procrastination fosters distraction. By splitting a big endeavor into smaller ones, procrastination can be defeated. Instead of diving headfirst into a massive task, driving oneself to do smaller ones is easier. Break up your time wisely if you struggle to complete your work or studies. Consider taking a 10-minute break after 45 to 50 minutes of work. According to studies, regular breaks might improve productivity and information retention. Even a little motivation may go a long way. Setting up a reward system is a smart move to encourage yourself to finish a task. For instance, reward yourself if you finish an essay without interruption.

Form routines to block out distractions and maintain focus. Working longer hours doesn't always lead to more done tasks. Be wise and maximize your time as work expands to fill available time. Our minds are programmed to save energy, so avoid distractions and prioritize tasks. The fact that most individuals are not particularly clear on their goals is a major source of distraction. Your daily thoughts should primarily focus on accomplishing your goals, and most of your effort should be directed in that direction. Be very clear about your direction and final destination. I advise evaluating your goals and assigning priorities for the completion of each. A major distraction is paying attention to the negative opinions of yourself and others. As your mind is renewed through the word of God, you will conquer your negative thoughts and see yourself as God sees you. However, you will have to handle the negative opinions of others.

DEFY NEGATIVE THOUGHTS

Negative thoughts can factor in low self-esteem, downheartedness, stress, and social anxiety. Understanding how you think currently (and the issues that occur) is the key to changing negative ideas. After that, utilize techniques to alter these thoughts or lessen their impact.

Our thoughts affect how we feel and act since our thoughts are connected to our emotions and behaviors. The Bible teaches in Philippians 4:8 to fix your thoughts on what is true, honorable, right, pure, lovely, and admirable. Think about things that are excellent and worthy of praise. Therefore, even if you occasionally have negative thoughts, it's crucial to know how to prevent them from ruining your day. 2 Corinthians 10:4-6 (ESV) reads, For the weapons of our warfare are not of the flesh but have divine power to destroy strongholds. We destroy arguments and every lofty opinion raised against the knowledge of God and take every thought captive to obey Christ, being ready to punish every disobedience when our obedience is complete.

You can improve your self-awareness and become more cognizant of your thoughts by engaging in mindfulness practices like meditating on the promises of God recorded in the Bible. Thinking-stopping meditation helps us discover the truth and understand how others' thoughts affect us. Avoiding negative influences like biased news and opinions can help maintain sanity and distance oneself from harmful thoughts.

DECLUTTER YOUR ENVIRONMENT

Declutter removes clutter from a place to organize and prioritize your commitments, calendar, material possessions, etc. Your thoughts can be more orderly in a decluttered environment. It would be best to abode by a few basic guidelines to declutter your life successfully. Be practical first. You won't be able to finish your house all at once. Research indicates that decision fatigue sets in when we make more choices, and we can become more impulsive or avoid making any decisions. Second, divide the task into doable components. To avoid becoming so overwhelmed that you give up, you might only work on one drawer or closet at a time or allocate a certain amount of time, like an hour.

Sort first and arrange afterward is the third and most significant rule. It makes no sense to organize items you intend to discard. That is a waste of time and mental energy! Last but not least, take the simple course of action first. Luke 12:15 (NIV) gives the words of Jesus. Then He told them, "Watch out! Be on your guard against all kinds of greed; life does not consist in an abundance of possessions". Making simple judgments first gives you the psychological benefit of dealing with less information, lowering your decision, burden, and stress level.

A cluttered bedroom will affect the quality of your sleep. Numerous advantages of getting enough sleep include improved mental health.

Sleep deprivation can make you tired and harm your ability to think clearly. It interferes with brain cell transmission, causing momentary memory loss. Make getting a good night's sleep a top priority if you want to start clearing your thoughts and forming good habits.

Exercise is good for your whole mental health in addition to your physical health. Regular exercise improves focus and mental clarity while lowering anxiety and depressive symptoms/thoughts flooding your mind.

Allow yourself time to unwind and relax, even for a brief break. Meditation can help clear your mind and improve focus. Listening to relaxing music can also help. Spending time in nature can reduce anxiety and depression. Writing down thoughts and feelings can create a space for problem-solving and self-exploration. Journaling can be therapeutic and help organize thoughts.

You can win the battle of your mind by consistently organizing your priorities and keeping the focus to finish each task, protecting your mind, overcoming distractions, defying negative thoughts, and decluttering your environment.

Dr. Phyllis Fuller

Dr. Phyllis Fuller is the founder of Kingdom Dominion Apostolic Network (KDTN), SOAR School of Ministry, founding Apostle of the Gathering for the Ambassadors of Jesus Christ (Church) in Houston, Texas, and Author of The Calls of God to Ministry. As a Prayer Coach, she builds and establishes Intercessory Prayer Teams across the earth.

She instructs and hosts Prophetic Internship, trains on Spiritual Warfare, how to serve on an Apostolic Team, Prayer, Power of Purity, Praise, and Worship. She is a committed ambassador dedicated to Jesus Christ and resolute to equip and prepare His people for the work of the ministry. Dr. Fuller has dedicated her life to her Kingdom of God mandates.

She holds a Doctor of Theology Th.D., BarnHam Graduate School and Seminary, and a Master of Art (M.A.) in Christian Counseling American Institute for Christian Education. She is an anointed and gifted vessel with 30 years of continuous apostolic work.

Her Motto is "If I am known, I want to be known for making Jesus known."

She is a proud Mother, Grandmother, Spiritual Mother, Mentor, and Friend of God.

The Consequence Of Spreading Myself Too Thin, Taking On Too Many Battles By Mary Davis

I am excited to be in this anthology to encourage others to learn from my mistakes. I beat myself up because I did not prioritize my battles. I did not know we could not fight everyone else's battles alongside our own.

So, I had to understand the power of self-preservation. I realized my battles involved taking on the community or environment I was mentioned in. Watching my mom helping others throughout my life made a significant impact. I became the jack of all trades, a master in juggling tasks. I am so guilty of taking on too much at one time. At first, it seemed manageable, and it used to take a lot to break me. The deadline in this book proves I am spread too thin; I would stop one project and start another and miss the deadline.

Now I am frustrated, my hair falling out, and I feel shame. Since I did not follow through in a timely manner, this can wear on your self-confidence.

I had reports due at church, chapter due, and community scheduling; there goes overkill. This became a nightmare, with no clear focus due to the project timeline. The church treasurer and financial secretary gave up their position, and who else is the only one (trustee) dumped in my lap? Lastly, my daughter's driver did not show up; I felt obligated to help her get patients to their appointments.

Yesterday, I fell asleep at 4 in the evening, woke up at 7:30 p.m., and thought it was the next day. This is, in reality, too much for anyone to take part in daily without organization. This is a significant risk to my health and many other factors. In my dilemma, you see no organization skills or delegation of duties.

Now, I know self-care is necessary. I can step back and appreciate the body God gave me. Self-care: sometimes, we ignore our bodies by what we eat; we are unbalanced in our lives and not fulfilled at the end of the day. I felt guilty because someone came and asked for help or got into a battle, and I thought I should help them so they would not hurt or be confused. I forgot about myself; my life is not balanced and fulfilling when I lack proper self-care. My health is in jeopardy because I am taking over someone else's battle. You always feel sick, irritable, and anxious; everything is a chore. So, it is not selfish. It is just an act of loving myself, empowering myself, and being aware of my surroundings.

You will end up with high blood pressure, and they will still walk around healthy with no problems because you took on their problem, so you get all the problems that come with it. Focus on issues that align with your values and principles, and know what you want to accomplish. There is danger in spreading yourself too thin; you can encounter stress and irritability. This is major here: no time for yourself and activities you love and need so much. Not enough sleep. Lord, inability to concentrate

How you engage in your battle is especially important. Never engage in something that will leave you frustrated. Trust in the Lord with all your heart and lean not unto your understanding; he will direct your path. I learned that people worry more about you turning it over and letting it go. You cannot take time back. It took years to find this out. Don't let a false sense of responsibility drain you. Say no in a season of change and growth is wisdom.

I am writing this chapter in the 9th month, a season of rebirth and a shift. Thank you, Lord. You must let God sift you to be ready for that shifting man. First of all, we must be comfortable in saying no. Do not feel guilty Because you observed things that were not ethical or transparent. Sometimes, you feel trapped in your obligation, but saying no would not carry your burden. Do not bear the false sense of responsibility that would drain you. Hey, man

Finding out which battles to fight or ignore is critical to having a successful business, relationship, self-improvement, health, physical energy, and mental awareness. The most important thing I have learned is time; you cannot get it back once it is gone. Most business suffers due to a line of planning and flexibility, which stagnates growth. When it is time to look at my situation, I am not focused and procrastinate.

PRIORITIZING MY BATTLES

I realize when she leaves other people's life challenges alone, there Is less mental worrying. I found out everything takes time and energy. It is not always who wins, but did I make the best use of my time?

When I look back, tomorrow is not promised to me, a life worrying about grown family members and their problems, their kids, just a battle I do not need to get involved in; the family should be love and camaraderie. Arguing on different issues of no concern or family or business is unhealthy, especially if you cannot do anything about it.

People will think you do not care or seem cold, but we must start asking, is this important? Do I need to deal with it? Can my time be better spent elsewhere? Strategies were identifying battles that contribute to personal growth. We must explore the consequences of spreading ourselves so thin that taking on too many battles is what happens.

When you take on too many battles, the extra thing turns out to be bigger than expected. Chances are the quality of delivery drops. They will be put on a shelf, and sometimes, with the help of procrastination, you forget that you did not take care of your business. You are more involved with their situation than they are, and the most unrewarding thing is that after you put all your time and energy into someone else's battle, they do not even take your advice.

People will look at you crazy, but you must prioritize with the understanding that self-improvement is #1. The second thing is recognizing the importance of setting boundaries and learning to say no. The main reason it is so important to prioritize is that helping friends and family can also be detrimental. I found I can maintain healthy boundaries and relationships with others and be more committed to the things to say yes to. Since I struggle with saying no, I have learned a firm no without an apology works. Learn to step back, see if this is worth my time, and let it go.

Be prayerful and mindful of what our physical and mental health could be at state. I found out that spreading myself this thin is within my control.

I will stop taking on additional duties and make sure I have enough time and staff. Do not give time and energy to other people's priorities.

PRIORITIZING MY BATTLES

In this time, we need a more balanced and empowered life.

If you have any of these symptoms below, it is a sign you are spread too thin.
- Lack of the ability to concentrate. Everything feels like a priority, which makes it hard to zero in on one thing.
- Always falling behind. A backlog can make it hard to catch up.
- Always feeling sick, irritable. This causes me to work with regret, no joy in doing what I love.
- My days are blurred. Small tasks seem huge; the whole day is full, with little accomplishment.

Here are some of the reasons I was spread too thin.
- I did not have enough committed help. Reliable help is a sure way to get things done.
- Everyone comes to you to help solve their problems.
- Never want to let you down. I used to want to be a people pleaser.

- Chaotic workspace and mind lead to clutter.
- Knowing your limitations. I was working a whole day; very little was my work. Now, I am okay with not doing it all.
- Organization helps keep your day on track, and I feel I have accomplished some of my tasks.

I will leave you with this: learn how to delegate your tasks/duties as it will organize your life. A plan and daily activity book will keep your stress down with a scheduled pan. This can be a long, hard-to-reach child.

Mary Davis

Mary Ellen Davis is a dedicated community advocate and volunteer who has spent over 40 years serving the St. Louis community. Originally from Memphis, Tennessee, Mary graduated from Hamilton High School and later relocated to St. Louis, where she obtained an Associate Degree in Diet Technology from St. Louis Community College of Florissant Valley. Alongside raising her family, Mary actively volunteers in her community.

Mary's volunteer work began with Acorn Housing for the Homeless, which inspired her to initiate the Blessing Bag initiative. She has been a member of Mount Esther Missionary Baptist Church for over 40 years, actively participating in the Mass Choir, serving as a Sunday School Teacher, and contributing to the Trustee and Deaconess Board.

For more than 25 years, Mary has been a member of the Federation of Block Units of Metropolitan St. Louis, an auxiliary of the Urban League of Metropolitan St. Louis. She has held various roles within the organization, including the Area F Council Chair for the 1st, 2nd, and 27th Wards. Currently, Mary serves as the Financial Secretary and Membership Committee Chair.

Recently, Mary was elected as the Committeewoman of the 27th Ward. This position enables her to empower her constituents by providing valuable insights into city offices and emphasizing the importance of their vote in shaping the community.

Mary has received several awards for her dedication to the Saint Louis community, including the S.P. Stafford Award from the Urban League of Metropolitan St. Louis, the Harper's Cup from the Federation of Block Units of Metropolitan St. Louis, and the Earl E. Howe Community Service Award from the 27th Ward. In 2020, she received Community Recognition from the Top Ladies of Distinction, Incorporated, and Special Recognition from Pastor Johnathan Lewis of the Saint Mathew Lutheran Church of the 27th Ward for participating in and supporting their 120th Anniversary Celebration.

In addition to her community work, Mary authorizes two new books. Her first book, "Navigating the Challenges and Opportunities of Raising Children Today," is filled with insightful reflections and practical advice for parents. It provides valuable guidance on parenting in today's world. You can get your digital copy of the ebook here: [Ebook link - https://amzn.to/42RVdo2].

Additionally, Mary has created an Activity Book designed to make the parenting journey fun and engaging. Packed with interactive prompts and creative activities, the "Navigating the Challenges and Opportunities of Raising Children Today Activity Book" is a valuable resource that promotes bonding and learning between parents and children. It offers an enjoyable way to navigate the challenges of raising children in the modern era. Grab your copy now: [Activity Book link - https://amzn.to/3MjCNY2].

To pre-order Mary's books or contact her, email her at Merryd543@gmail.com or purchase through the provided Amazon links.

Prioritizing You While on The Frontline of the Battle
By Shanice Murphy

Battles are conflicts or disagreements that can be internal or external with multiple individuals. They are fought with a specific objective to accomplish or to gain a sense of control. In the military, battles are fought between two opposing parties to gain control of territory, resources, or some other political goal. During these battles, those on the frontline are usually the leaders who are considered more skilled and responsible.

We all play a leadership role in life, whether in our profession, as a parent, or one who inspires others in the community. As one who leads, it can be difficult to put yourself first and choose your battles wisely when you are used to being at the forefront of all the battles. A healthy leader prioritizes self-care to be the best version of themselves to serve better those they're called to reach. We have to change our mindset and perspective to know that putting ourselves first does not mean to the detriment of others. We must water our own garden before we can be great in the roles God has placed us in.

We are often faced with daily, monthly, and even seasonal battles. These battles can be internal within ourselves, in relationships, or in our careers. It can be hard to put yourself first when you are the leader and responsible for the well-being of others. As a quick personal story, I remember when life became overwhelming with all the responsibilities and roles God had given me. It became so bad that I went into a deep depression because I did not properly prioritize myself and the battles that were important for me to fight alone.

I tried pouring from an empty cup, depleting me with no true energy to fight alone. I continued to try to put everything and everyone first until I had nothing left to give. It took a health care professional becoming very stern with me saying they did not care about what I had going on in life and their job was to ensure I was back to 100% first as a healthy individual. What good are you to anyone if you can't be good to yourself? This is the question I was left to ponder.

As Christians, God reminds us in Ephesians 6:12 that we are not fighting in the natural but against spiritual principalities. To do so, we must put on the full armor of God, including:
- Belt of truth
- Breastplate of righteousness
- Shoes of the peace
- Helmet of salvation
- Sword of the spirit
- Shield of faith

When covered with God's full armor, we are preparing ourselves for any spiritual battles that may come our way. Deuteronomy 20:4 says that God will go before you to fight your battles. I know you may be asking, but when do I sit back and let God take full control of a situation? The following are just a few ways to know when to let go and let God fight your battles:

- When you feel lost and confused.

- You become mentally and physically exhausted.

- You've tried multiple fights your way with no true victories.

- You feel there is no other hope.

Once you let go and let God, this does not mean to do nothing but to know he is in control and to let Him lead the way instead. These are steps you can take once you let go and let God take over:

- **Prayer and Surrender.** Pray for forgiveness and ask God to take over in the area or situation you can no longer control. Surrender it all over to him and faithfully pray over the situation.

- **Seeking guidance from scripture.** Find scriptures that speak to your battles in your time of devotion and meditation. Read scriptures that tell of His character and His promises to us. That way, when God speaks, you will know what's true and when to take action.

- **Having faith and trust in him.** When we relinquish all control over to God, we must fully trust and believe He will handle the situation as He knows best. God handles our battles differently than we may handle them. Faith is not to doubt nor question God's work, for his plan is bigger than ours.

- **Let go out of control.** As natural-born leaders, those who are used to fighting on the frontline, it can be hard to let go of control, but once you learn when to do so, it can be a sense of relief.

- **Practice patience.** Patience is no easy feat. It takes a lot of practice and unlearning behaviors. The most important thing about patience to remember is what you do and your attitude while you wait. Learn new skills and focus your attention on other things.

- **Take action.** While God takes over, there are still things he will require you to do in the meantime. You have to be ready and prepared to move when He says go.

- **Seek support and community.** You're not on the battlefield alone! It's important to have a support system you trust that can help hold the weight while you wait. Your support system can offer love, guidance, and prayers.

- **Maintain a positive mindset.** It can be hard to remain positive during a battle, especially when results are not right away. Staying positive makes the journey more bearable to continue.

- **Be open to hear and obey God.** Posture yourself to hear God clearly and be open to what He decides to do to win the battle. Winning the battle may also mean losing something we may have valued but no longer serves us. This will require us to obey God's will and put what we thought was best to the side.

Once we have Let go and Let God prioritize our battles, we must embrace resiliency and adaptability. We must continue to identify what battles we fight and those we hand over to God to fight on our behalf. Prioritizing those battles means we must effectively assess and manage them. Everything comes with a cost. The question is, what can YOU afford? Whether it be a career, relationship, or lifestyle change, nothing is worth giving up your physical, mental, emotional, or spiritual well-being.

When feeling overwhelmed with life's challenges, we must stop and save ourselves first by taking accountability in knowing when to go forward and fight versus when to stop and be still. Often, we play a part in our suffering by staying in situations/relationships that no longer serve us, especially when God has opened the door to escape. Yet, we stay for the sake of familiarity.

My prayer for you today is to take one thing from this chapter and apply it to your life. I pray that you know you are not alone with whatever silent battles you may be fighting. The victory has already been won, and you are a conqueror. You are courageous, strong, loved, important, and blessed. God never promised the weapons wouldn't form, just that they wouldn't prosper. Leaders are called to do mighty work but not always alone. Continue to seek God in your journey to identify your battles, prioritize them, and know which ones to hand to God. Stay encouraged, and know you were "built for this!"

Acknowledgments

I would first like to thank God, who is the head of my life. I am nothing and can accomplish nothing without Him. I want to thank my parents for raising me into the woman I am today and always supporting me in life. I want to give honor to my spiritual leaders James and Pamela Williams, for your support and guidance over the years.

To my little brother, you keep me leveled and inspire me every day. I want to thank my Aunt Stephanie Gore and the visionaries of this book for giving me this opportunity to be a part of such great work. There are a host of family and friends who have been with me along this journey in life, and I am forever grateful for my village. Last but not least, I want to acknowledge my son Bryson who has been God's greatest gift to me! Son, you motivate me every day and bring me such joy in life. I love watching the world through your eyes. I pray that this chapter inspires you and that you continue to push forward in life. This is just the beginning of God's purpose for my life as an upcoming author.

Shanice Murphy

Shanice Murphy is a native of Wilmington, NC, but resides in Columbus, GA. She is a believer in Jesus Christ, a true worshiper, and considers herself a multifaceted creative. Shanice is a Nationally Certified School Psychologist currently practicing in school systems within Middle Rural Georgia. Her work in mental health aims to support children, families, and systems to help children succeed academically, socially, behaviorally, and emotionally. She has served on numerous boards in leadership positions and has countless hours of volunteer work. Outside of her many roles and responsibilities, her most important role is being a mother to one amazing son she adores. Her goal is to create a platform and brand that glorifies God, inspiring others to have a personal relationship with Him. Although her passion is in child development, she wants to help women become their best selves by knowing their identity in Christ and prioritizing true self-care. In her free time, she enjoys reading, cooking, dancing, traveling, and spending time with family/friends. Although this will be her first book chapter in an anthology, God has given her the vision to write many books. Shanice aims to create a life that she does not have to vacation from serving her community in various capacities and leaving behind a legacy.

To connect with Shanice, email m.shanice77@gmail.com or follow @Sheispsyched on Instagram, Twitter, and Facebook.

Riding Through the Storm
By Sandra (Sandy) Johnson

Life is unpredictable. So we go about our daily lives never expecting to be blindsided or knocked backward two steps after making great progress and strides to achieve our goals. (Whatever that looks like) Whether it is a new job, business, or relationship. Oftentimes, we are hit with unexpected circumstances that shake our entire world. A curve ball that throws us off course, and we're ready to slap somebody into next week. But we must keep moving by faith, take a closer look at the circumstances, and ask ourselves a few questions.

1. How did this happen?
2. Was this God's doing?
3. Was this the right timing?
4. How can I move forward from here?

2 Corinthian 5:7 says, "For we walk by faith and not by sight." Whatever you set out to do, know that Faith without works is dead.

I'm SURE MANY OF YOU CAN RELATE TO what I'm about to share with you, especially if you're in ministry. So, hold on and ride with me through a season of my life that I believe will help someone at the end of the day.

In 1993, I married a Man of God who walked in the five-fold ministry with gifts. The first year of our marriage was very challenging, but I was determined I would stick with him because that's what we are supposed to do as a wife. We had moved nine times in one year from a hotel to a friend's apartment, and from one house to another, from renting a house next door to a crack house in a drug-filled neighborhood to renting a family member's house.

Through all this moving, I had to carry a large fibroid tumor – one the size of a grapefruit, two the size of a golf ball, and several small ones on the outside of my uterus, that was considered a high-risk. It was very, very uncomfortable. I had to totally depend on God. I often prayed and asked

God for instructions and clarity on what to do and when. I got a release to see a doctor and had prepared myself for the unknown. I discovered I was three months pregnant during the exam and didn't know it. What a surprise! Since I had large fibroids, aborting the child was suggested. Some felt it was the right thing to do and that I would be able to have more children. I didn't give it a second thought; I would not give up my firstborn; the devil is a liar!

Often, I felt so uncomfortable as I tossed and turned throughout the night to the point I had to take oxycodone to ease the pain. The only comfortable bed type was a pillow top or a water bed with body pillows in the front and back. And yes, those pills knocked me out! LOL.

I'm reminded of the scripture in **Jeremiah 29:11, "For I know my plans for you, saith the Lord. Plans of peace and not evil, to give you an expected end.**

As time passed, my husband was led to start a ministry, and I assisted him whenever possible. I truly believed I could be a pastor's wife, but something wasn't right. I began to question myself: do I have what it takes, what is expected of me, and

I hope I don't have to fight anybody while coping with these fibroids? Thankfully, I was able to work as I depended on God to carry me through. I often thought about my mother being in the position of a Pastor and how the experience was both good and bad. I was ready to tell a few people off who offended her, but she would always tell me not to worry about it and that she would take it to God in prayer. While in ministry, I had to remain close to home while my husband would be on the road ministering. So, I continued to pray and seek God for clarity, healing, and protection.

It's a fact that ministry comes with challenges for those who hold a position as a Pastor's wife, a church pastor, or other leadership positions. You may experience members favoring the Pastor while indirectly overlooking the Pastor's wife, which both should be treated with the utmost respect and honor. I've learned that too often, the First Lady is mistreated by the church members, and some seem to believe the Pastor would be better off with them, so they work to sabotage the marriage that God has ordained for ministry. (Go figure!)

The constant battles in our lives come to make us stronger and wiser. So, when we're confronted with these challenges, you must always be prepared and spiritually equipped as the scripture says in **Ephesians chapter 6:10-11, "Finally my brethren, be strong in the Lord and in the power of His might. Put on the whole armor of God so that you can stand against the devil's schemes**....

And you can rest assured knowing that God has your back as it is written in
II Chronicles 20:15, "Be not afraid nor dismayed because of this great multitude; for the battle is not yours, but God's.

In this season, we must know how to prioritize our battles. During one of my doctor visits, I was reminded that I was high risk, but I believed God was in total control of my situation. Hearing the doctors say that my baby could be born with Down syndrome and spina bifida can bring fear to anyone, but I refused to accept their reply and held onto the report of the Lord where His word says, by His stripes, I am healed. The enemy was really trying to plant a negative seed of doubt and fear into my spirit, but I wasn't having it. I continued to stand on the word of God and trusted Him to bring us (me and my baby) through this ordeal.

During my last trimester, while on our way to church, I experienced dizziness and faint while attempting to get out of the car. My husband began to pray this cute prayer, and I told him it was not working, and I started drifting away, lost consciousness, and stopped breathing for about three minutes. Somehow, I realized I was in a dark, quiet place. I couldn't hear anything or see anything. What a scary place to be!

I finally regained consciousness as I heard my husband call out my name and began to cry. It was the most terrifying moment anyone could ever experience. The paramedics were there when I came to, and I was able to translate exactly what happened to them. Sitting in the back of the ambulance, they continued to ask questions like, are you in any pain? And I answered, no I am not in any pain. After the Paramedics took my vitals, they concluded that everything was good, and they couldn't explain what happened and why. Thankfully, I didn't have to go to the hospital and was released immediately.

PRIORITIZING MY BATTLES

When you are already faced with unexplainable battles, you must trust God through every moment. And when it seems that people are coming against you and your marriage, and sometimes the battles can occur within your marriage, let them know that you are prioritizing your battles, and you can't afford to fight them, too.

After writing this chapter, I had a dream while taking a nap. In that dream, I was riding through a storm. I was on a large ship and ended up in a life raft. The water was calm initially, but then the waves began raging. While riding the waves, I looked to my left and saw the waves were getting bigger and bigger as the lifeboat was being tossed to and fro. I looked to my right and saw theater seats flowing by me in the opposite direction, and I thought I was going to collide with it, but I didn't. (Thank you, Jesus) I began to call on the name of Jesus as the waves were getting stronger and higher. I had to hold on to what looked like a white sheet, and the other end of the life raft was rising out of the water. I noticed a large ship passing by me, and I realized then that I was somehow moving through the waters in an area where it was calm and safe out of the raging water and on solid ground.

I noticed a high-rise building and a three-story building on both sides of the waters I had just flowed out of. I ran into one of the buildings to call someone to come for me, but I didn't have a phone; then I woke up. I hope this chapter encourages you and reminds you to put your trust in God as you prioritize your battles and say to the devil, I can't afford to fight you too while singing this song by Douglas Miller, "My soul has been anchored in the Lord."

Sandra Johnson

Sandra Johnson (Adkinson) is the youngest of seven siblings and is survived by three. She has one adopted son, two biological children, and two grandchildren. In 1980, Sandy graduated from H.D. Woodson Sr. High School and joined the armed forces a year later. In 1990, Sandy served in the US Army Reserve for eight years with an honorable discharge. Sandy was a Statistical Assistant contractor, Data Entry Clerk, Medical Facility receptionist, Administrator Assistant, File Clerk, Staff Assistant, and Home Healthcare Aide

SANDRA (SANDY) JOHNSON

(voluntarily). Sandy served as Pastor of a Women's ministry and counselor. She attended the Kingdom School of Ministry under the teaching of Dr. Cindy Trimm and graduated with a certificate of completion. Sandy served in her church in various roles, including Concierge, Usher, Intercessor, Audio Assistant, Video Assistant, and Praise & Worship team. Sandy is always willing to serve in any capacity, wherever needed.

Contact Sandra:
Email. sjohnson9711@gmail.com
FB: Sandy Johnson
IG: sjdiamondangel

Balance in the Battle
By Dr. Stephanie Gore

All major battles mark a turning point. So, how do we find balance in the battle at a turning point? I declare this turning point to be the place of victory. The place of victory is the same as the battle in your mind. Balance in the battle is the realization that you've already won. God has declared you to be victorious in him! Not losing balance is acknowledging God, putting him first, trusting the process and the one who promised. Speak the word of God in season, out of season, when you come, and when you go.

Balance in the Battle requires focus and unwavering faith. I'm encouraged by Peter's faith to believe and to try, "For as the body without the spirit is dead, so faith without works is dead" (James 2:26). I can't imagine what he felt in that moment, leaving the boat to walk towards Jesus on the water. Faith is to believe the impossible, to receive the intangible, to see the invisible, and to stand firm on the eternal hope of God's love and provision. How challenging it is to choose faith over fear.

As a woman, mother, entrepreneur, and leader, trying to juggle many different roles requires making myself a priority. Learning to manage my time, set healthy boundaries, and establish realistic expectations has allowed me to maintain a balanced life. Before that self-realization, there was a recurring cycle of self-inflicted mental wounds. Mental wounds of thinking that prioritizing myself was a selfish act rather than a selfless act. Here's the plan that helped me walk step by step into victory.

Seven steps to victory:
1. Set your mind on things above!
2. Guard your heart.
3. Spend time in preparation.
4. Gird yourself with truth.
5. Avoid unnecessary conflict.
6. Bridle your tongue.
7. Find your battle buddies (tribe).

Set your mind on the things above! "Finally, brethren, whatsoever things are true, whatsoever things are honest, whatsoever things are just, whatsoever things are pure, whatsoever things are lovely, whatsoever things are of good report; if there be any virtue, and if there be any praise, think on these things" (Philippians 4:8). Take authority over self-defeating thoughts, discouragement, and unbelief. You have the authority through the holy spirit to subject distressing thoughts to dissipate.

"Casting down imaginations, and every high thing that exalteth itself against the knowledge of God and bringing into captivity every thought to the obedience of Christ" (2 Corinthians 10:5). Replace negative thoughts with faith-based positive affirming thoughts that align with God's will and his word. In Proverbs 23:7, Soloman shares words of wisdom, "As a man thinketh in his heart, so is he."

Guard your heart! Begin by asking God to search your heart, for the hidden things of the heart may hinder your ability to maintain balance. "Create in me a clean heart, O God, and renew a right spirit within me" (Psalm 51:10). The right spirit and a renewed mind create endurance in the battle. King Solomon said it best: "Above all else, guard your heart, for it is the wellspring of life" (Proverbs 4:23). Consider King Jehoshaphat's response when facing battle. He proclaimed a fast for all of Judah and sought the Lord. Seek the Lord before seeking the advice or counsel of man. And when support is needed, use discernment to choose who you can release your heart to. Evaluate your person and test the spirit they operate in to ensure they honor the holy spirit. "Beloved, do not believe every spirit, but test the spirits, whether they are of God; because false prophets have gone out into the world" (John 4:1).

Spend time in preparation. "Study to shew thyself approved unto God, a workman that needeth not to be ashamed, rightly dividing the word of truth" (2 Timothy 2:15). The living word will be a light unto your path and a compass to guide you. During the battle, it is not the time to rely on your strength, knowledge, or intuition. Devote time to prayer, fasting, and communion with God. And when you lack understanding, seek him, and he shall be found. Ephesians 6:11-13 tells us how to prepare, "Put on the whole armor of God, that you may be able to stand against the wiles of the devil.

For we do not wrestle against flesh and blood, but against the rulers of darkness in this age, against spiritual hosts of wickedness in the heavenly places." Even with a busy schedule, prioritizing preparation time helps maintain balance.

Gird yourself with truth. To grid means to prepare yourself for something challenging. "Therefore, gird up the loins of your mind, be sober, and rest your hope fully upon the grace that is to be brought to you at the revelation of Jesus Christ" (1 Peter 1:13). To gird the loins of your mind with truth sets you free from the tactics, traps, and ambush of the enemy. "Behold, you delight in truth in the inward being, and you teach me wisdom in the inmost place" (Psalm 51:6).

Avoid unnecessary conflict. Disengage from internal and external conflicts and choose not to accept invitations to conflicts involving others. Ask these three questions before giving time, space, or energy to situations or events.

Q1: Is this situation or event caused by my choice or behavior?

Response: If you can identify that you are the problem, it is not the time to delay repentance during a battle. Be reminded that we are not in battle with one another. Ephesians 6:12 reminds us that "we do not wrestle against flesh and blood."

Q2: Did this situation or event occur because of a lack of boundaries?

Response: Unhealthy boundaries within interpersonal relationships will lead to unresolved conflict. This is a distraction and contributes to a lack of accountability for change. Remember that conflict may develop when implementing healthy boundaries, as the individuals who most benefit from the lack of boundaries will not embrace the changes well.

Q3: Is this situation or event caused by misunderstanding or miscommunication?

Response: Make no room for pride in the battle. If you can acknowledge it, then you should quickly seek to resolve it. "Let your speech always be gracious, seasoned with salt, so that you know how you ought to answer each other" (Colossians 4:6). And when misunderstandings occur, hasten to self-correct faulty thinking and assumptions about the intentions of others.

Bridle your tongue. Shh! "The Lord will fight for you, and you have only to be silent" (Exodus 14:14). When you know God is fighting your battle, you speak differently. Every thought shouldn't be spoken. Everything you notice shouldn't be pointed out. Pray for the discernment to know when to speak and be silent. But never allow the balance to silence your praise. Keep praise on your lips! As this is your greatest weapon! And likewise, when you speak, speak with wisdom, acknowledging that your tongue is a weapon that can wound others. "Death and life are in the power of the tongue" (Proverbs 18:21).

Find your battle buddies. God will not leave you alone! "I will never leave you, nor forsake you" (Hebrews 13:5). He will equip you to maintain balance in the battle! Even when you acknowledge the weapons that have formed, remember the promise that they will not prosper. "No weapon that is formed against thee shall prosper, and every tongue that shall rise against thee in judgment thou shall condemn" (Isaiah 54:17). Battle buddies will not be on the battlefield comparing battle wounds. Battle Buddies understand the assignment and will remind you of yours!

Seven Affirmations and scripture readings for daily balance.

1. My mind is set on things above.
    - "Let this mind be in you, which was also in Christ Jesus" (Philippians 2:5).

2. My heart is filled with perfect love.
    - "There is no fear in love, but perfect love casteth out fear: because fear hath torment" (1 John 4:18-19).

3. I am ready, prepared, and equipped NOW!
    - "Being confident of this very thing, that he which hath begun a good work in you will perform it until the day of Jesus Christ" (Philippians 1:6).

4. I embrace truth and repel ALL evil.
    - "Flee the evil desires of youth and pursue righteousness, faith, love, and peace, along with those who call on the Lord out of a pure heart" (2 Timothy 2:22).

5. I align with God's order and purpose.
   - "Many are the plans in a person's heart, but the Lord's purpose prevails" (Proverbs 19:21).

6. I have self-control and exercise it daily.
   - "But I discipline my body and bring it into subjection, lest, when I have preached to others, I will not be disqualified" (1 Corinthians 9:27).

7. I have an ordained circle of support.
   - "Whoever walks with the wise becomes wise, but the companion of fools will suffer harm" (Proverbs 13:20).

Finding balance in the battle includes some losses and often facing uncomfortable truths. It was difficult for me to take the losses and declare it my winning season as it felt like a contradiction. I had to grasp that the promises of God may not always make sense at the moment but are spoken as an act of faith. Hebrews 11:16 serves as a reminder, "And without faith, it is impossible to please God because anyone who comes to Him must believe that He exists and that He rewards those who earnestly seek Him." How often have you found yourself seeking God during tough battles? Learning to seek Him earnestly includes the times when we aren't battling tough circumstances or situations. If you do something earnestly, you do it in a serious, heartfelt way. In consistently doing so, it builds our faith and confidence in God.

The dictionary defines confidence as "faith or belief that one will act correctly, properly, or effectively." What happens when we lose confidence in the Lord when facing a battle? We may grow tired or weary right before the victory is won. Some scriptures encourage us to keep our confidence during the battle. Hebrews 4:16 points us toward God's grace, "Let us then with confidence draw near to the throne of grace, that we may receive mercy and find grace to help in time of need."

What a good, good God that we serve who provides a way of escape to ensure that we maintain balance. He calls us friend! 1 John 5:14 reminds us that we can ask God anything, "And this is the confidence that we have toward him, that if we ask anything according to his will, he hears us." And be reassured that the Lord will uphold you, "For the Lord will be your confidence and will keep your foot from being caught" (Proverbs 3:26). The Lord that promise will be your defense, shield, and protection to cover you in battle. Stay under the cover and forge forward in fortitude with confidence and reassurance that you've won the battle.

Acknowledgment

To my amazing sons, Mark Alfred Gore, Jr. and Marcus Alfred Gore, my greatest lessons learned were through parenting, but mostly listening to you. I fought my greatest battles on my knees and prayed that you wouldn't have to.

Dr. Stephanie Gore

The most impactful patrons of a society needing abstruse mending are those equipped with unyielding notions of benevolence and boldness, capable of shifting atmospheres. Fashioned with this exact essence is the compassionate international best-selling author Dr. Stephanie Gore.

Dr. Stephanie Gore is a therapeutic doyen, coach, and CEO and founder of Optimistic Solutions Counseling Services, LLC and Step2it Network, LLC, two business conglomerates specializing in private practice counseling, corporate-mandated anger management, as well as the provision of online career advisement, counseling, and coaching, through education and motivational interviewing. Having more than 15 years of perspicacity in a diversified range of clinics, social services, vocational services, and much more, Stephanie is a proven asset in her field and a trusted partner in the healing processes of vast clientele.

Her mantra is clear: Stephanie believes people can be empowered and equipped through optimism to promote lasting change for a brighter future. With that intent, she aims to empower, equip, and uplift others through positive regard and self-awareness, proving that positive change is attainable.

Stewarding a full-time consociation with excellence, Stephanie shares a sincere regard for education, achievement, and community involvement. She received her honorary doctorate degree from Harvest Christian University and earned a commission for chaplaincy licensing. She also received her master's degree from Troy University in Counseling and Psychology. She is a Licensed Professional Counselor, National Certified

Counselor, Certified Rehabilitation Counselor, Vocational Expert, and Anger Management Specialist III (Fellow). Adding to her tenure in advising and educational consulting, Stephanie is recognized by the National Anger Management Association (NAMA) for her extensive work in anger management and emotion regulation.

When Stephanie is not out being the change the world can feel, she is an asset to her local communal body and a loving member of her family and friendship circles. Stephanie has accepted the call to marketplace ministry as founder of Reprieve Us Again Global Impact, a non-profit organization with the mission and passion to provide mental respite through education, training, coaching, and outreach.

Dr. Stephanie Gore. Leader. Advocate. Humanitarian. Author. Speaker.

DR. STEPHANIE GORE

To connect with the author:
https://linktr.ee/stephaniegore
Email:
Stephanie@Optimisticsolutionscounseling.org
reprieveusagain@gmail.com
Website: www.optimisticsolutionscounseling.com
https://step2itnetwork.com

Getting To Know God
By Sarah McLean

One day, my Mom and I were conversing about knowing God. It sparked my desire to have a deeper relationship with God. Knowing *about* God was not sufficient. I disclosed to my Mom that something had happened to me. I did not feel as connected to God. Was I missing something? Had I lost faith? Was I mad with God because of the things I had gone through? Perhaps I was angry about the things I was currently going through. The reality is that it was a combination of all of the above and more.

After our conversation, I continued to think about getting to know God. I did not want anything to be in the way of our relationship. That connection was necessary for my life. I prayed, repented for my anger, and so much more. I cried, and I cried until the tears stopped flowing. I could only sit and suck in the air like a little child. As I sat there with staggered breathing, I knew things had to change. I resolved within myself to chase after God. I was determined to know and trust in God! I was not ready for the events in my life God used to help me to know and trust in Him.

My career has been unique in healthcare. I love helping others. Along my journey, I realized that I also loved to educate others. A door that I had waited on for years opened for me. My excitement was palpable. Not only was I able to educate, but I was also able to travel across the United States. I was so thankful to God for this awesome opportunity.

Work was going well, and I was relatively busy. God had answered my prayers. Prayer and diligent study of His Word continued. Then, seemingly out of nowhere, everything began to fall apart. It felt like a tsunami had hit my life. Work was being cut back, and my compensation followed. Bills began to fall behind. Instead of feeling like I was growing closer to God, I felt like I was failing. Were my prayers and study of God's Word not enough? I resolved not to give up. I continued to attend church, pray, and study God's word.

While I was going through what I called a crisis, I was not the only one. This was during a time when many people were losing their homes, or they were struggling to pay their mortgage. America was in a crisis! I did not know what to make of all of this. I was experiencing all sorts of emotions. What could I do to make things better? My journey to know God did not seem like a positive one. It was not fun. I thought things should be going well because I was doing something good. Right? My desire for more of God did not cease. I was not going to back up, give in, give up, or retreat. The objective was to keep moving forward.

One day, I received a notification in the mail that the county was having an event for those having problems with their mortgage. There would be mortgage companies and others present. This notification arrived just in time. I was one of the ones having problems with my mortgage. I was thankful. God had heard my prayers and opened a door for me. Things were going to work out.

Early that Friday morning, I arrived at the facility. It appeared many people had the same idea. The line was long. I took my place and stood in line with my paperwork, a 16-ounce water bottle and no money in my purse. I was unsure of the amount of time we would be there; I hoped my water would last because I did not see a water fountain. No matter what, I was determined to remain until there was a resolution to my situation. The hours ticked away slowly. We stood in line for hours. Some people were called to go to different areas, while others were told to remain in line. I wondered when they would get to me. I remained hopeful.

Mortgage companies and resource agencies worked hard to assist all attendees. Many walked out with good reports, while others did not. My hope began to increase. Some came by to report their situation was too dire for help. Things had gone too far. I said a prayer for them.

Hours trickled by as morning turned into afternoon and afternoon into evening. We had been standing for hours. My water was gone. The line had decreased. When was my turn coming? Finally, my name was called. Yes! The opportunity to speak with my mortgage company had finally arrived. It was after 5 p.m. My heart was filled with joy.

The mortgage representative offered me a seat in front of his computer. He introduced himself as one of the managers. Oh, yes! I was speaking with the right person. He took my paperwork and looked at his computer. He reminded me that I was two months behind and that it was about to be three months. I was well aware of my situation. The mortgage company and I had spoken several times.

    The manager looked closely at his computer and said I had been enrolled in a government mortgage program. I politely said, "No." I had previously contacted the mortgage company to be in this program and was denied. No explanation was given. The manager and I went back and forth a few times as he tried to tell me that I was in the program. I remained steadfast and continued to tell him, "No." Suddenly, he saw something on the computer and said, "No! You are not in the program." Hearing this, I did not know what to think. I became more alert. Was he going to help me get into the program offered to countless Americans during this mortgage crisis? I waited for some positive news.

    Sitting patiently in the chair, I considered how good it felt to sit for a few minutes. Suddenly, those thoughts ended. The Manager's countenance and attitude changed right before my eyes. He looked up from his computer. With piercing eyes and a chilling voice, he proclaimed with emphasis, "We are going to foreclose on your home!" A chill went down my spine. I felt like he had gathered some rocks and put them in a boxing glove. Then he punched me in the face with the fastest jab ever. What just happened here? I did not have time to bob or weave. He continued, "It doesn't matter if you give us a check for the entire amount; we will still foreclose on you!" The impact of his words was massive. There was no compassion. All I could do was listen.

I would love to say that I began praying and worshipping God then. No. That did not happen. I was stunned and in shock as he then skillfully dismissed me. I gathered my face and papers, smiled, thanked him for everything, and rose from the seat. The strength to get up and walk away did not come from me. There was no one else to see, so I exited the building. It was now after 6 p.m. on a Friday. There was nothing I could do!

On my way to my car, I saw one of the persons who was in line with me. They asked me how it went. I let them know no one was able to assist me. They attempted to provide an encouraging word. As I walked, I felt a different type of strength inside me. It was unusual. I realized that I was actually at peace. There were no tears. I went to the car and drove home. Those words continued to play in my head, but only for a brief moment. I was so calm. I wondered why I was so calm. It was a bit scary. Was I going home and having an adult tantrum and pity party? I arrived home safely and still calm. Those events never took place. What I did know was that no one could help me except God! I could not ask anyone for the money. His words were clear. Somehow, I felt covered and comforted. There were no words. There were things about God that I had to learn. So many things were happening alongside this event, but I did not feel overwhelmed. How could this be?

  Monday morning was business as usual. My assignment was out of state. I was teaching a very early class for the night shift staff at the hospital. After class was over, I checked my phone. There was a voicemail from the mortgage company requesting a returned call. I did. I was only able to provide my name, and the conversation ensued.

The person on the other end of the phone was very kind and began to tell me why they had called. The caller told me they had a plan for my mortgage. Foreclosure was never mentioned. All I had to do was agree to the terms over the phone, and the paperwork would arrive for my review and signature. WOW! All had turned around since Friday evening. I owed it all to God! No one else could do it. Literally! Things had worked out for my good and God's Glory! Only GOD!

Explaining to others what had happened was beyond my capability. All I know is that I began to feel my connection with God change. My trust in Him solidified. I started to know God in a way I had never known. I wanted Daniel 11:32b (NKJV) to be my life's mission, "but the people who **know** their God shall be strong, and carry out exploits." I understood an exploit to mean *a bold or daring feat, a notable, memorable, or heroic act.* (Merriam-Webster Dictionary) What a memorable moment! I knew God was with me. I felt His love. He was my provider, problem solver, and protector. He fought for me! No one could tell me any different. I did not have to ask anyone if He was there. I was grateful for what God had done. I had to put my

PRIORITIZING MY BATTLES

pink hand wraps and boxing gloves back in the closet to allow the greatest fighter to fight on my behalf!

Psalm 103:7 (NKJV) says, "He made known His ways to Moses, His acts to the children of Israel." This speaks about relationships. Moses had a relationship with God. Moses knew God. That is what I am striving for. I want to know God, not just know *about* God. I want to know God's character, nature, presence, and ways. I knew I could not piggyback off someone else's relationship with God. No one. Not my Mom's, Pastor's, or my neighbor's. I needed to know God for myself.

When we meet someone we are interested in, we spend time getting to know them better. We learn their ways, their character, and their nature. You can tell when someone only knows *about* a person. They know very little, if anything at all. It is the same way with God. You can tell if someone truly knows God or if they know *about* God. They repeat what they have heard others say but cannot give you one scripture to substantiate what they are saying. You don't want to know people better than you know God. Why put in time getting to know others and no time for God? You want to know God so well that when you speak of Him, others are persuaded they want to know Him.

In this age of social media, many people have lots of followers. It looks as though they know a lot of people, or a lot of people know them. The truth is when you sift through the followers, there are only a handful that know them. Some know *about* this person, while countless others have no idea who they are. They wanted to join the crowd. Many see God like this. Only a few truly know God. Many know *about* Him, while others are trying to connect to those who **know** God. I want to know God for myself. Join me on this journey – *Getting To Know God*. We will never know everything about God. He is bigger and deeper than we can comprehend. Let's take the time to build a relationship with Him. It is worth it! Get to know Him! I am glad I did. I am Sarah with "H."

In His Grace,
Sarah McLean

Acknowledgment

To the One who fights for me, Our Father. I am thankful for the many battles you have won. Thank you for loving me. My love for You grows stronger each day. I am forever in Your care.

To my Mother, the late Mrs. Esther M. McLean, thank you for all the thought-provoking conversations that ignited my desire for more of God. To my family and friends, thank you for your continued love and support.

Sarah McLean

Sarah is the youngest of four children. At an early age, she had a deep love for God. As a teenager, Sarah dedicated her heart to Jesus. She loved reading God's Word and still does.

Sarah especially loves traveling, shopping, reading, attending theatrical productions, sporting events, and trying new restaurants. She believes in living life to the fullest. Her primary love is to serve God and His people. Helping others is what prompted Sarah to become a Registered Nurse. She has been commissioned as a Faith Community Nurse and received a Master of Divinity and a

Master of Practical Theology. Sarah is currently working on her Doctor of Philosophy in Christian leadership. In addition, Sarah has served as a Chaplain.

Sarah continues to seek to please God in all that she does. Fulfilling the call of God upon her life is paramount. Her greatest desire is to hear the Lord say, "Well done, My good and faithful servant." (Matthew 25:21)

Stop Fighting Yourself! Get Out of Your Own Way!
By N. Lynn Gobert

I can't recall how many times I've used the phrase "Get out of your own way!" THOSE WORDS SPEAK VOLUMES TO MY SOUL, whether I was encouraging someone else or myself. Being in your own way could resemble negative self-talk, low self-worth, and self-sabotage. Somewhere along your journey, you may have convinced yourself that you do not deserve all the good things life has in store. You tend not to know how to delight in a win when great things happen. Instead, you find a way to highlight failures by harping on how it could have gone better, or you might not celebrate the accomplishment at all. Although there is room for reflection, you must be deliberate about giving yourself constructive vs. destructive criticism. We are often very conscious about how we speak to others but don't consider how we speak to and treat ourselves.

By taking an interest in your contentment, you allow yourself to revel in your achievements and cheer for yourself. Changing how you see yourself and taking an intentionally positive approach to day-to-day living will help you defeat the idea that you are not good enough and catapult you towards a life filled with intentional purpose, gratitude, triumph, and a bright outlook on your future.

We were all created with a purpose but often lose sight and cannot fathom that we ARE who God has called us to be. Often, we won't forgive ourselves or others for past mistakes that may have negatively impacted our lives. I have found that sometimes, it seems easier to forgive others than it is to forgive myself. Forgiving yourself calls for you to permit yourself to move forward after taking accountability for where you have fallen short. But there is a distinct difference between holding yourself accountable and holding yourself back. If you hold yourself accountable, you can use every situation as a lesson learned regardless of the outcome. You hold yourself back by allowing negativity to creep in and cast a dark cloud of uncertainty over future endeavors before they even come to fruition.

Unforgiveness keeps us from healing from our past disappointments and keeps light from penetrating the darkness. The Bible says in Proverbs 3:5, "When you doubt yourself, you can trust the Lord for direction." God wants us to be confident in knowing that He will guide our paths even when we are unsure. With that said, if God is leading you, get out of your own way! We are meant to thrive in this life and not operate in a constant state of survival. True happiness starts from within and begins with how we think of and speak to ourselves.

Cynical or self-deprecating thoughts about oneself are known as negative self-talk. This includes engaging in a never-ending psychological conversation with yourself where you continuously focus on your flaws, failures, or shortcomings. This type of self-talk can diminish your self-esteem, decrease self-confidence, and negatively affect your overall well-being. Identifying and countering negative self-talk with a healthier self-image and positive affirmations is imperative.

One way to defeat negative self-talk is to practice self-compassion. Give yourself the same grace and understanding you display towards others. Be kind to yourself, especially when met with disappointment and difficult situations. Another way to counteract negative thoughts is to be attentive when negative thoughts come into your mind. Be sure to consider what triggers led to the rise of these negative thoughts and feelings. Being aware gives you insight into avoiding certain situations that may cause your thoughts to turn negative. When you have a negative thought, challenge it by asking yourself if there is evidence to support it or if the thought is irrational.

Attempt to replace negative thoughts with positive ones. For example, if you think, "I'm never going to get this right", replace it with, "It may take some extra effort, but I CAN get it done!" Knowing that you don't have to face negative thoughts alone is also important. If you need help processing your thoughts, you should try talking to a close friend, therapist, or counselor to seek a different viewpoint and recommendations on how to move forward. Take each day one at a time and continue developing your positive self-talk tool kit, trusting the process and yourself.

Life experiences and lack of emotional support can contribute to low self-worth, especially if you have experienced early childhood trauma, neglect, emotional or physical abuse. This life-altering event could also take place throughout adolescence and adulthood. Although it may take some intentional soul-searching, low self-worth is not a permanent state of being. You can work towards rebuilding your self-worth through self-awareness, establishing support systems, and committing to self-care routines. Identifying contributing factors and seeking help can be critical steps toward increasing self-worth. Much like negative self-talk to counter low self-worth, you can make deliberate adjustments by challenging negative thoughts when they arise and replacing them with positive affirmations. Instead of emphasizing your weaknesses, focus on your strengths and prioritize keeping a visual aid or list of your accomplishments to assist in reaffirming your capabilities.

Setting realistic and attainable goals can also help motivate you to move forward with plans.

Another way to boost your self-worth is to surround yourself with people who encourage and support you. Attach yourself to hype women and men who build you up, and don't allow you to be too hard on yourself. Think of them as your cheer squad who root for you as you play this game called life, celebrate your wins with you, and encourage you to keep going when you're faced with losses.

It is also imperative that you silence your haters! Distance yourself from individuals who are negative and don't add value to you, as they can make it more difficult for you to see the positive side of situations. Always remember that increasing your self-worth will take persistent effort on your behalf. Give yourself ample time and grace to foster positive change on your journey towards achieving high self-worth.

Have you ever been involved in a smear campaign sponsored by yourself? Self-sabotage is like having a former teammate join an opposing team and bring with them your playbook! It's funny how we must fight harder than ever in a world full of nay-sayers! Between television and social media, society's version of normal and what it means to be beautiful and successful is distorted and can contribute to negative perceptions of ourselves. You can get in your way by self-imposing obstacles that keep you from reaching your goals and telling yourself you can't do something before you even try.

Self-sabotage can look like procrastination in starting a task that you know is important to complete, self-destructive habits, and thoughts that hinder you from moving toward success. For instance, a fear of failure can be debilitating if you allow negative thoughts to consume you and cast doubt on your abilities to the point that you never move forward with the project. Self-doubt can be lies you tell yourself, such as not doing something is better than failing at an attempt to do it. These thoughts are subconscious attempts to undermine the reality that you should strive to do your best and turn your failures into lessons.

When you have convinced yourself that you can't achieve a goal, then, in turn, you don't achieve the goal; you are reinforcing negative thoughts, which can lead to a vicious cycle of more self-sabotaging habits. I too have allowed my fear of failure to hinder me from making the most of opportunities. When I was in my mid 20's I had a fear of public speaking. To counter my fear, I decided to join the Toastmasters Club on base. I really enjoyed learning the art of public speaking and the speeches that were given by fellow club members during meetings. Although intrigued, I was only half invested. I allowed my anxiety to keep me from volunteering to give a speech and prompt me to exit the club to avoid being asked.

Luckily when the next opportunity to dive into public speaking presented itself it was a mandatory requirement for promotion to the next rank. The Air Force sends Senior Airmen, and newly selected Staff Sergeants to Airmen Leadership School (ALS). ALS is designed to develop supervisory and leadership skills, which include public speaking.

During the 6-week course, I had to prepare several speeches for course credit. Like Toastmasters, speeches were timed and graded based on how well the speaker performed. I was nervous and found myself speaking so fast that I ran out of breath. However, after each speech, I gained more confidence in my ability to speak to a room full of people. By the end of the course, my anxiety had subsided, and I was speaking with ease. I have since volunteered to emcee numerous events, facilitated trainings, and given briefings to high-ranking leaders in the Armed Forces.

You can break free from self-sabotage by stepping into your greatness! Don't allow the failures of the past to keep you from achieving new heights in your personal or professional life. Use your life's experiences and knowledge to debunk the negative thoughts as they enter your mind. Encourage yourself!

Here are a few tips that can assist you in your efforts to live a more positive life. Believe in yourself and put your oxygen mask on first! How can you add value to others if you struggle to add value to yourself? Take care of yourself first by establishing positive self-perception and echoing positive affirmations daily to combat negative thoughts. Fight against the spirit of self-doubt and push yourself past the test to the testimony. If you ever find yourself in a standoff with yourself, call in reinforcements and ask for help. Be it a trusted friend or a medical professional, build a team of supporters who can help you through difficult times.

You are worthy! You can do it! You ARE who God says you are! And there are no limits to the success you are destined to achieve if you simply GET OUT OF YOUR OWN WAY!

Acknowledgments

Lord, I thank you from the bottom of my heart for your faithfulness, mercy, and unwavering love. In this season, your goodness is running after me! I give you all the glory and honor, knowing that I am nothing without YOU! My heart is FULL!

To my children, Messiah, A'Mya, and Omega, you are my greatest inspiration. I'm proud to be your Mommy! Your endless curiosity and creativity remind me daily of everything that is good in heaven and on earth. Your belief in me is unmatched and means the world to me!

I am immensely grateful to my beloved family and friends, whose unwavering support and understanding make it possible for me to live my purpose and chase my dreams. Thank you for your patience, motivation, encouragement, and countless crying/laughing sessions that helped me on this journey.

To my mentors and peers, thank you for pouring into me! I am dedicated to paying it forward.

With love and appreciation,
Norma Lynn Gobert

Norma Lynn Gobert

N. Lynn's life is a testament to service, leadership, and perseverance. As a mother of three children, she balanced the responsibilities of parenthood with an illustrious 20-year career in the U.S. Air Force, where she rose to the rank of Master Sergeant. Her expertise as a Health Services Manager was complemented by a Professional Manager Certification and Associate in Healthcare Management from the Community College of the Air Force, further highlighting her dedication to the field. During her military career, she was certified as a Victim Advocate, Resiliency Training Assistant, and TeamSTEPPS Instructor, dedicating on and off-duty time to supporting Airmen and continuous process improvement within each organization she was assigned.

In addition to her military career, N. Lynn has ventured into entrepreneurship as the owner of **Infinite Possibili•Tees Inc.**, offering custom apparel, reflecting her creative spirit and determination to promote resilience and encourage others that the "sky's the limit". She is leaning into the gifts that God has given her and pursuing her purpose by standing up **On Purpose Community Outreach Development**, a nonprofit organization embodying her passion for servant leadership and fostering a positive impact in the community she resides.

N. Lynn is deeply purpose-driven, constantly seeking ways to fulfill her mission of "Get everyone to the brightest point of their Light, Build the Kingdom, and Give God Glory." She is dedicated to mentoring and empowering others, providing them with the encouragement and guidance they need to reach their fullest potential.

Her tenure as an Airmen Medical Transition Unit Flight Chief fueled her desire to advocate for Armed Forces veterans, ensuring the well-being of service members. Her strategic thinking significantly improved the quality of healthcare services provided to servicemen and women under her charge. Her current role as a Human Resources Specialist for the Department of Veterans Affairs affords her an opportunity to continue to serve the nation's heroes and their families.

In every aspect of her life, N. Lynn is a shining example of selfless service and a commitment to making the world a better place. Her journey is a testament to the power of determination, leadership, and a heart that beats for others.

Personal Email:
nlynn.ministries@gmail.com

Infinite Possibili-Tees:
www.infinitepossibilitees.com
Email: infinite.possibilitees1@gmail.com

On Purpose Community Outreach Development:
Email: onpurpose.cod@gmail.com

Prioritizing My Battles: I Cannot Afford to Fight You Too
By Roschelle Taylor

For a long time in my life, I found myself feeling like there was a void or emptiness. I would wake up each day motivated to go through my daily scheduled plans, not realizing that the things I thought would complete me were not found in my job or my own. Abilities, through things, through people, or any other sources. It was revealed that I sought things that could not sustain me in every area of my life. What I searched for could only be found through a graceful and merciful God.

I needed an authentic, cultivated relationship with God through the Holy Spirit. It was. Through this relationship, my purpose was revealed. I didn't know that the longing I felt was because I needed to agree with a loving God and

Holy Spirit that Jesus told us through the Word of God that He had to go away for the Holy Spirit to be made available to me.

    I was allowing the battles (that I created) in my life to control me, my emotions, and how I responded to good and bad circumstances. I had to allow the Holy Spirit to transform my old thinking through the washing of the Word of God. I had to turn my total being over to an Omnipotent God who knows all. Who was and still is well able to stand in the gap for me and fight for me. A God who was my present help during times of trouble and uncertainty. A God that never left me or forsake me. Before, I was moving and operating as a defeated/imposter. Position of faithlessness, but I was telling myself I was good.

    There came a time when I understood that there was only one way to move past what I had put myself through completely surrendering my will for the Will of God. I had to come to an agreement with God and the Holy Spirit to know and understand the plan and purpose for my life. I had to get to a place and space in God where I could truly say that I was in complete alignment with God to receive the manifestations through the

Word of God; I had to trust GOD for everything, no matter what it felt or looked like. I had to allow the scriptures I was reading to become more real than the emotions I felt, the thoughts I was thinking, and those unfiltered choices I was making. I had to increase my faith and understand the scripture in the book of Romans 10:17, that Faith comes by hearing and hearing by the Word of God. I had to be the hearer and the Doer of the Word. So, I began to feed my Spirit.

I sought after the conferences, the revivals, and the other services that help. Water and build up my faith, but I also had to increase my knowledge and understanding through the Holy Spirit. Jesus died so I could be engrafted (rooted and planted) into the Kingdom of God, giving me the rights and authority I needed to stand when I had done all to stand. I had to develop and cultivate a relationship with God and the Spirit. This relationship completely shifted the trajectory of my life and my mindset. I was heading for self-destruction through sabotaging behaviors. I was fighting battles because I was receiving and accepting outcomes based on what I felt and what was comfortable. I had to sit with the choices and the decisions that I was making that seemed like the best things for me at that time. Some ways seemed right and good, but the end almost destroyed me and kept me from receiving all God revealed for my kingdom journey. But Holy-Spirit.

My indicator light on the inside of me shows Himself mighty in my life. He began to fill the void where I no longer longed for people and unhealthy things. He began to show me where I needed to set healthy boundaries; He helped me to renew my mind and to check my heart posture. He taught me things I needed to know about myself, not my thoughts and perceptions, that were at God's discretion. He began showing me how to further the ministry for my life. He showed me that I had to be willing and obedient to the things of God. I had to diligently seek Him for instructions on pursuing Him for clarity in situations and the directionality this gave.

I had peace because I understood whose strength and authority I utilized when facing battles. This peace is not as the world gives. It speaks to me, and my Spirit can bear witness with the peace and the peace givers. It can only be found in God through the Holy Spirit. The missing link was connecting the Word of God to my life. I submit unto you that a relationship with Christ would fill the emptiness in your life just like it filled the void in mine. Now, I can prioritize my battles and place them where they need to be so I can fight the God fight of Faith.

God was speaking, but I wasn't always postured to hear and listen efficiently or effectively. The WORD of GOD had to be planted, watered, and increased by God. God had to show me through the Book of Luke 10:38- 42 that I wasn't prioritizing my battles; I was creating battles that I wasn't ready to fight, some of which I wasn't supposed to fight. More importantly, I needed to get in a place and sit in silence to hear what the Spirit of God was trying to reveal to me. I had become a Mary when Martha was who I was being called to be. I had to take on the ownership (characteristics) of who I was through the lenses of God the Father.

I had to submit to all that God was presenting before me. I had to remain focused on the things pushing me into my next. I was no longer seeking, searching, and running all over the place to get the right Word when God showed me what I needed to do to transform my life. I no longer was moved by my emotions and started conducting my life according to what God said concerning me. I released the self-sabotaging behaviors that were blocking me from prospering in the things of God. The battle with myself, my way of living, and my inner me held me hostage, but God said I come that you may have life and have it more abundantly.

God accomplished the journey to locate my authentic self for God. For that, I thank my Lord and Savior Jesus Christ. For He is the author and the finisher of my faith. I had to learn that the process of becoming who I was called to be had a prerequisite attached to it that required that I be completely grounded, submerged, and anchored in the Word of God to be commissioned to tread and rule over what God has instructed me to rule over, I had to understand that this is not a one and done. I will always have to prepare myself daily to meet the challenges I face so that I don't find myself discouraged in the very season of my life that could catapult me into my next.

I had to invest in myself to ensure that I was better than the day before in all areas of my life.

PRIORITIZING MY BATTLES

That is how I will make sure that I leave nothing undone. I had to learn when and how to engage in the battles approved by God (to build and protect me) and those strategically developed by the enemy (to annihilate or take me out) and use them for my demise. (failure). Then, I had to release the ones I created to God so He could work them out for my good.

God purposefully set me up for a comeback in a battle that could have crippled me, but instead, he placed me in a state where I could recover and be made. Whole. A place where I could birth the very thing that could have been aborted had I not—allowed Him to take over and nourish me to a place of sustainment. A place where I could draw the strength to move forward to get to my expected end.

In Matthew 22:14 reads for many are called, but few are chosen. I am choosing to answer the call to be a chosen one by God.

Roschelle Taylor

Roschelle is the author of the book From the Bedroom to the Throne Room, Is it a Love or Lust Relationship that focuses on being delivered and set free by the restoration power of the Word of God. She is an entrepreneur of Global odor- eliminator products. (X-IT Global) which removes unwanted odors by annihilating the source. She served on the City Council as a dedicated community leader who built strong, positive relationships with the City Council members and her local community of Charlotte,

Tennessee. Roschelle is a life-long educator dedicated to shaping young children's minds and providing environments conducive to and supporting lifelong learning. She has a B.S. in Education from Tennessee Technological University and a M.S. in Education Science and Theory from Arkansas State University. She believes in building strong, meaningful partnerships with parents and the school community so that effective teaching and learning can be at the forefront of the learning process.

Contact information:
Email: rtaylor9391@yahoo.com
Facebook: Roschelle Taylor
Gmail: roschelletaylor70@gmail.com
Instagram: @roschelletaylor

Every Battle Is Not Mine
By Dr. Janice Grier

Sometimes, we find ourselves fighting battles that don't belong to us or trying to fix other people's problems. Then, we get overwhelmed with problems that we choose to take upon ourselves, and we find ourselves in an area of aggravation and frustration! We have to learn to let people fight their own battles in life.

My motto is: If we lose too many Battles of Life, We will lose the War!

That's why we must prioritize our battles before trying to help others fight theirs. I can't afford to fight someone else battles because mine need attention! I found out that every battle is not mine to fight! I am not a Fixer! I am not usually the one that handles people's problems and responsibilities. It took me a long time to comprehend this life lesson, but I learned it the hard way through life experience.

About ten years ago, while in a Pastoral role, I felt like I had to fix everybody's problems with which I came in contact in the ministry. I began to take on battles that no Pastor or Leader should take on; I found myself trying to fix problems that did not belong to me and found myself in a place of depression, discouragement, and confusion because they were not my battles. I couldn't fight them in my frame of mind, so I began to talk to God in sincere Prayer! And God told me, why are you bringing these problems to me that they won't take the time to talk to me about? God spoke to me and said this is not your responsibility. People will let you take on their problems and walk away and leave you struggling for your life under the pressure of their battles that they will not take the time to fight!

So, I prioritize my position as a Leader and ask God's forgiveness for taking on battles that distracted me from hearing His voice! When we realize we are taking on battles that are not ours, we must immediately start prioritizing what to fight and what not to fight; we must do this to protect our peace of mind and be able to hear God!

PRIORITIZING MY BATTLES

I have learned over the years that every battle is not mine to fight! So now I can choose my battles in my Home, Ministry, and Business. I choose not to have my mind cluttered with things or people that will cause me Stress or distraction from my assignment with Christ Jesus. I realized every day that every battle is not mine to fight." every day, I keep my mind clear by reading and studying God's word and working on a daily productive Prayer life to keep my relationship with God.

Sometimes, we have to stop and take another look at the situation that people are going through and realize we can't fight and win that battle because it's not yours. God has given us the Power of choice; let's use it wisely in taking on others' responsibilities and Issues. Protect your Peace of mind and your ability to hear God clearly in the trying times because, as I stated before, every battle is not mine to fight.

Chief Apostle Dr. Janice D. Grier

Chief Apostle Dr. Janice D. Grier received Christ into her life at 14. She graduated from Newton County High School with honors. She then attended Georgia State University, completing her degree in 1975. She continued to pursue her education at Dayspring Theological Seminary in Panama City, Florida, and graduated in 2002.

Apostle Grier is spiritually motivated to work in the Kingdom. In 2007, she formed Reach Beyond the Break Outreach Ministries, a community outreach program that assists with food, clothing, housing, and utility assistance.

God shifted the ministry's name in 2009 from The Fellowship Church of Praise Atlanta to the New & Living Way International Deliverance Ministries, Inc. In 2010, after serving in God's Kingdom for 44 years, God elevated Pastor Grier to the office of Apostle.

In 2010, Apostle Grier started the J. Grier Christian Academy in Tucker, Georgia; it is licensed and incorporated by the state of Georgia. The J Grier Christian Academy is now J Grier Child Development Center, open during spring and summer breaks, offering summer educational services for youth.

In May 2011, Apostle Grier made her presence known on Channel 57 T.V. Comcast Channel 2 airwaves. Apostle Grier's first book, "How to Graduate from People College," debuted in January 2015. This must-have book is available on Amazon.

Apostle Janice Grier has received many awards, including the 2015 "Kingdom Woman of the Year" award from A Woman of Worth

Empowerment Ministries, Kansas City, Missouri. In 2016, she received the "A Woman of Worth" award from Deborah's Daughter, Inc. She was recently awarded the 2018-2019 "Kingdom Educators INSPIRE" award from the New and Living Way Youth and Community Outreach Department.

Apostle Janice Grier was elevated to Chief Apostle in 2015. In 2018, she was awarded an honorary doctorate from the School of the Great Commission (SOGC) Bible College in Columbia, S.C. She is now Chief Apostle Dr. Janice D. Grier.

2019 Apostle Grier returned to academic study at The School of the Great Commission Bible College and Seminary and earned her Doctor of Theology degree. In 2020, the National Association of Christian Counselors certified Dr. Grier as a licensed Christian Counselor. She is the Dean of the Greater New and Living Way School of the Great Commission Bible School and Seminary in Tucker, Georgia. Additionally, Dr. Grier is the CEO of the J Grier Community Development Center in Tucker, GA.

Chief Apostle Janice Grier is an anointed woman of God and has been chosen to walk in the five-fold ministry. She moves in the areas of healing and deliverance. Many people have been healed from terminal diseases and lifelong illnesses and delivered from bondages in other areas.

Chief Apostle Janice Grier stands firmly and walks boldly as a Kingdom 'dominionaire,' a vessel of great faith and authority. She is truly a mother in Israel. She oversees the New and Living Way International Fellowship Connections, 12 churches under Apostle Grier's leadership, covering three nations: the United States (Georgia, Alabama, Missouri), Kenya, and Uganda (Africa). As God continues to speak through Apostle Grier, she moves expeditiously, taking quantum leaps and bounds through faith. Her goal is to bring God's people into the maturity of Christ so that they may walk in a 'New and Living Way.' Apostle Grier humbly states, "After 56 years, I am still a FAITH-WALKER, and I am STILL excited about GOD'S NEXT!!"

An Unwavering War
By Gwendolyn E. V. Monroe

When a Queen of leisure awakes every day, she sips tea and adjusts her crown, whereas we of a royal priesthood awake to adjust our armor to fight a never-ending war. We fight this war tenaciously! We fight daily!

Good versus bad, Satan versus Abba *(Our Heavenly Father)*, flesh versus spirit, truth versus lies, and positive versus negative. We have been forewarned that we WILL experience some battles/troubles in this world and our lifetime. Those tests and trials will come to make us stronger. The key to being an overcomer is prioritizing the battles within the war from the perspective that, tedious or not - we KNOW we WIN!

Let's return to where it all began when we said 'YES' to Abba! A process akin to when I was inducted into the United States Army in December 1971. Our one YES to Abba was us spiritually raising our hands to be sworn into the Army of the Lord, the Army of the Most High God, the Army of Abba—an Army whose mission is to build and solidify His Kingdom here on earth.

We are all aware every army consists of soldiers committed and contracted to fight for the cause, the mission. The Army of our Lord is no different and has **Soul.jahs**™ who were sworn in via a spiritual covenant to fight for the cause of Jesus Christ. Abba has His part of the covenant, which ONLY He can do, and we have our part - that He absolutely WILL NOT do!

I remember when I answered the call to join Abba's Army. Some of my friends and family members didn't understand the change they saw in me. Honestly, most of the time, even I didn't understand how my likes and dislikes were being altered. The one thing I was sure of was that my relationship with Christ had priority over all other relationships – and thus, the first battle was revealed. It's relationships that make the world go round; mine now were viewed through the lens of Christ. I was no longer a soldier in man's army but now a Soul.jah™ in Abba's Army. Abba desires complete control of my soul (mind, will, and emotions), so I had to learn a new set of 'rules of engagement.'

Over time, I realized who I was and whose I was! Above all else, I know that I AM His Soul.jah™ *(a warrior with covenant continuous confidence in the cross)*; I KNOW my assignment *(determined awareness of and spiritual steadfastness to)*; Abba has called me to WAR *(radical unabated obedience)* and Abba has called me to WIN *(faintless unfaltering faithfulness)*. It's all about our Lord and Savior and His Kingdom. Everything that we 'say' *(words)* and everything that we do *(actions)* has an impact on the Kingdom of God.

So, what does it mean to be a Soul.jah™ in Abba's Army - I'm glad you asked! Let's look at three basic battles I believe every Soul.jah™ will encounter because of their divine Y.E.S.

1. **Assess** whether you have loaded the correct ammunition (Are your words and actions consistently positive and fruitful?) *[2 Timothy 2 and Galatians 5]*

As Soul.jahs™, we are issued ammunition (ammo) specific for the type of weapon Abba has called us to be. The fundamental ammo we are all issued are words. As citizens in a voice-activated Kingdom, we must know what is in our arsenal and how we use this ammo. Reading and understanding the Word of God is the greatest source to replenish our ammo supply. His Word is sharper than any two-edged sword, and He watches over His words to perform them.

As a Major in the U.S. Army, I carried a Beretta M9 9mm pistol. To dislodge the bullet, I applied pressure to the trigger, causing the bullet to be released from the chamber and travel through the barrel to exit from the muzzle. The wrong ammo in my weapon may have caused it to jam or misfire, resulting in personal harm. This seldom occurred because I was very familiar with my weapon.

Words are the spiritual ammo we hide in the chambers of our hearts. They are hidden not only so we do not sin but also for Abba to use us as His weapon. If we don't have discernment and release a word too soon, it may backfire and/or become friendly fire because the intended recipient is not ready to receive it and will completely miss the mark. Abba's timing is the strategy we must consider before firing. Speaking too soon,

PRIORITIZING MY BATTLES

regardless of how right it may be, could be fruitless if our words fall on stony soil.

We must purpose to have the right words in our heart chamber so when the pressures of life squeeze, we can still release a timely word for the building of another Soul.jah™ and the Kingdom. We must ensure Abba is familiar with His weapon *(us)*!

Time has taught me to wait for the Holy Spirit to release me, allowing my words to bear fruit for the Kingdom and avoid friendly fire. Ensure you have the right ammunition when Abba reaches for His weapon *(you)* to enhance the effectiveness of His Army!

How? *Self-leadership* and studying to show yourself approved! If you keep the right ammo in the chamber of your heart, life can squeeze all it wants because nothing will exit your mouth, but the Word of God, and it will accomplish what and why it was sent - thus bearing much fruit!

2. **Decide** whether His weapon *(you)* is clean and well oiled (Is your heart clean and is there oil in your lamp?) *[Psalm 51 and Psalm 92]*

I was and still am quite competitive! When I went to the gun range to develop a relationship with my Beretta M9, I cleaned and oiled it before attempting to fire it. Even though I kept it stored in the unit's arsenal, the metal parts could rust and corrode just because of the environment of the storage area. My weapon performed best when I kept it clean and oiled. The extra cleaning was not mandatory by regulation; I made a decision to go in and clean and oil my weapon when I knew the unit was going to the range.

We make decisions every day, and the decisions we make control us. We decide ...what to believe, ...what to say, ...what to do! Yes, we decide ...who to like, ...who to talk to, ...who to trust! But, more importantly, the consequences of those decisions inevitably shape our lives.

Decisions control our lives, but what controls our decisions? The outcome of our lives is the sum of the consequences of our decisions. Once we have decided we can live with the consequences – deciding is easier!

You may want to consider these consequences before making your next decision:

    A. Will it move me toward my destiny?

B. Will it help me meet my goals?
C. Does it align with my values?
D. Does it meet a need that drives me?

Indecision is the enemy of success. The inability to decide is what causes us to get **StuckOnStop**™. I'll unpack that term on another day, but for now, make sure you are a clean and well-oiled weapon for Abba's use!

How? *Self-awareness* as your spiritual gauge! Know if your spiritual tank is full or empty. Running on empty is a danger to you and to anyone Abba sends you to. Whenever Abba reaches for His weapon *(you)*, you should be ready, in and out of season. You should be clean and well-oiled for whoever and wherever He desires to send you!

3. **Edit** to ensure you are His weapon of choice! (How well does Abba know you, and is He pleased?)

Suppose you don't like how your life is *life.ing*, then make the edits to have what you desire! Abba said He would be with us in the valley, but He did not say the valley would negate the mandate on our lives. We are called to please Him with our lifestyle. Our heart posture will help us walk by the spirit, not the flesh. Are you pleasing Him?

How do we know if Abba is pleased with us, or is it time to make changes for Him? Do we need to edit some things for our life's purpose? Let's take an introspective look at our spirit man by considering the following questions:

A. Have you surrendered everything Abba cannot use to be a weapon with clean hands and a pure heart?
B. How big is your faith compared to when you gave Abba your divine Y.E.S.? Has it grown because you exercise your faith? I'm just asking because the Word says, 'Without faith, it's impossible to please Him.'
C. Do you know how much you please, Abba?
D. Can you work diligently on a project without receiving accolades from men? Is that still small voice, that inner knowing enough praise for your job well done?
E. What does 'to the glory of God' mean to you? Do you consistently live this phrase?

Make sure you are walking by the spirit, so as not to fulfill the lust of the flesh.

How? *Self-identity* by truly knowing yourself. Be honest to identify and acknowledge your weaknesses. You won't pursue a solution if you don't recognize a problem. Offer your life as a pleasing sacrifice daily. *[Proverbs 8]* Obeying Abba's commands instead of following your desires is a pleasing aroma to Abba. *[Numbers 15 and Psalm 139]*

Can you afford to fight this battle? Is it worth it? Consider these Rules of Engagement:

A. The battle spoils must yield positive fruit!
B. The battle spoils must bring about growth consequences!
C. The battle spoils must result in edits that please God!

We swore into God's Army with one divine word - Y.E.S. We decided to yield our old ways and endure the process of surrendering our will for His Will for our lives.

Do you remember what you meant when you said Y.E.S.? My Y.E.S. meant firstly, I gave my word that I would **Y.ield** my mind and thinking to His instructions and ways. It was amazingly interesting to learn to give way to the arguments, demands, and pressures between the Word of God and my then stubborn way of thinking, but I said Y.E.S.! Secondly, I vowed to **E.ndure** the strenuous changes I knew were coming to align my will with His Will. To suffer patiently is to endure. When I tell you I was and still am allergic to the word patient, but I gave Abba my Y.E.S.! Then, thirdly, I promised to **S.urrender** my old emotions and actions to be renewed. This part is an incessant process, but I said Y.E.S.!

I don't pretend to suggest that this process has been easy, nevertheless it was my decision. Because I knew I could live with the consequence of it; I also committed to accomplishing my decision excellently. But wait... then, I read that Abba desires me to prosper, even as my soul prospers! WHAT!? I WIN!!!

We WIN this unwavering war when we learn to prioritize the battles as they present themselves. Each battle matures us just a little more; however *(comma)* we also live with an unwavering commitment to serve His Kingdom as a lethal Soul.jah™ in His Army!

The faith of Abba's Soul.jahs™ must be as unwavering as the war we fight daily! Join me, and let's continue to fight the good fight of faith and

B.E. Abba's weapons on earth – His weapon that won't drawback and won't backfire!

READY... **SET**... *let's* **G.R.O.W.** – *together*™!

Acknowledgments

To Abba, my Heavenly Father, for choosing me to use me for the building of His Kingdom.

To every tenacious man and woman who refuses to allow the lemons of this world to deny the fulfillment of their divine call.

To my mama, Hattie L. Williams, my shero! You continuously display empowering love. You epitomize uncompromising strength and tireless commitment fueled by your faith in Jesus Christ that you taught us.

To my Godmother, Gladys Turner. Your faith, resilience, and prayer anchor your unwavering spirit of conviction and love. I saw more than I heard you say!

To my village, friends, family, and saints whose paths crossed mine for a reason or a season to empower, inspire, correct, and push me forward!

Thank you ALL for your love and support!

Gwendolyn E. V. Monroe

Gwendolyn Elaine (Vaughn) Monroe was born in Kansas City, Missouri, as the fifth child to the union of Leo M. Vaughn Sr. and Hattie L. Jones. Gwendolyn retired in June 1993 after twenty-one honorable years in the United States Army as both an Enlisted Officer and a Commissioned Officer and continues to hold the rank of Major.

Her first book, "Yeah, I P.O.G.A.D. - don't you?" was released in 2001, and her first CD, "Doubly Graced" was released in 2009. She has a passionate desire to see others walk in their purpose and makes the time to help them 'edit' their lives so as not to employ their fear, but choose to F.ace E.verything A.nd R.ise (F.E.A.R.)

Education is one of her primary tenets, and she often says she could be a professional student due to her inclination to know and grow more. Her prayer is to remain humble and teachable, and she believes that what you don't know can hurt you. Gwendolyn has two AA degrees (Business Administration and Graphic Design) and a BS (Business Administration/Accounting) with plans to pursue her Master's. In June 2015, she received her Certification as a John Maxwell Leadership Coach/Trainer/Speaker and is deliberate in 'Growing Leaders'. She joined Your Small Business Toastmasters Club in December 2016 to become a better communicator.

Coach Gwendolyn, aka '**Meyjermom**™', is the AVO & Founder of genUwenGEMS LLC housing both SAYLAH Ministries International (SMI) and editingL.FE Enterprises (eLE).

Married for thirty-six years, the widow Gwendolyn has three sons (two daughters), nine grandchildren, and five great-grands who affectionately call her mom, mama, grandma Gwen, and GiGi. Gwendolyn lives life unabatedly, focused on serving her life sentence to **"Live my full potential – to die empty!"** Ready... Set... *let's* G.R.O.W. - *together*!

CONNECT with Coach Gwendolyn:
www.genuwengems.com
ask@meyjermom.com
404-903-1133 | IG/Threads: @askmeyjermom

Warfare With Guilt and Shame
By Dr. Evelyn Hill

When we hear "rape," we immediately picture a dark night, an empty street, and a stranger lurking around a corner, waiting for the right victim. So, we learn self-defense techniques and carry mace as protection, as we should. And when rapes happen in settings like this, we know what's happened and that it rightly should be reported to the police and the rapist sent to prison. Tragically, *73% of sexual assaults are perpetrated by non-strangers – people we know.* And *50% happen inside the victim's home or within a mile of that home.* [Source: New Hope Inc. at new-hope.org]

Shame and guilt are the twin towers of pain, two sides of the "less-than" coin. After sexual assault, it's rare to find a girl or woman who does not hold onto one or both.

I think of Natalie, who was raped by her mother's boyfriend when she was five years old. "I came away," she recalls, "telling myself how stupid I was to go upstairs when he called to me. If I hadn't been so dumb, this might not have happened."

Natalie took shame and guilt upon herself at *five years old*, even though she had done absolutely, unequivocally, categorically *nothing wrong*, and she carried that shame and unachievable determination to never make a mistake into her 50's, until she worked with a trauma counselor helped bring her into truth. Author Brene Brown talks about the difference between shame and guilt. Shame is a focus on self ("I am bad"), and guilt is a focus on behavior ("I did something bad").

Please hear me. I'm not saying there is no authentic, earned guilt for something we've done wrong. I break into your house and steal your valuables; that's just wrong. And if I feel guilt, it's well-deserved and intended by God to be a scratchy, miserable reminder of my need to make things right. That's healthy guilt. But oh, there exists an unhealthy, false guilt whose sister is a shame. Though we've done nothing wrong, we can be held captive to the sense that we *did* do wrong; we *are* wrong. And so very often, these devious and imprisoning sisters can keep us from living life in freedom and joy, even though they have no right to hold us.

Our society counts "rape" as that dark night-in-the-alley experience and has trouble validating improper sexual advances from a brother or an uncle or a family friend...or even someone we met online. Not welcome, yes, but calling it rape? Saying it could be as deeply painful as being preyed on by a stranger? How very often these two see an easy prey in those of us who have been raped. Somehow it was our fault; in some way, we did something wrong to bring this on. We deserved it. If only we had..., or if only we hadn't...

Sister Tamar

It amazes me how very true-to-life the Bible can be; no over-spiritualizing or churchy talk that covers wrong when wrong exists. Such is the case in the story of a beautiful young princess named Tamar, and her evil brother Amnon, told to us in 2 Samuel 13. Amnon, one of King David's sons, was Tamar's half-sister and fell in love with her. Beyond a simple infatuation, he longed for her day and night, enough so that a friend noticed his distress. The two of them then hatched a wicked plan intended to seduce Tamar. Amnon sent a message to his father, the King. "I'm sick," he moaned. "Please send my sister Tamar to cook for me." In a culture where men's requests, especially when they come with the weight of royalty, were seldom rebuffed, King David agreed and instructed Tamar to cook for her half-brother.

But a hearty meal was never Amnon's intent. Once the meal was prepared, he lured Tamar into his bedroom and forced himself on her. She protested, "Don't do this wicked thing!" But he didn't stop. And after the act, the Bible says, 'he hated her with intense hatred. In fact, he hated her more than he had loved her." And he ordered, "Get up and get out!"

When King David found out what his son had done, he was angry but did nothing. When Tamar's brother Absalom realized what had happened, he told her to be quiet about it, citing the family connection that would cause damage to the family name. So, Tamar carried the weight of this undeserved wrong. In those days, virgins wore special clothing to indicate their status; Tamar could no longer dress in this way. But she also couldn't join the company of married women, so the rape brought isolation and unmerited shame.

If I feel alone in shame or false guilt, I sometimes think back to Tamar. She did nothing wrong; indeed, she resisted her half-brother's attack to the degree that she could. But she left that day a humiliated woman. When she had come to Amnon's house a few hours earlier, she came as a beautiful princess, dressed impeccably, invited, sought after, valuable. But after she left in disgrace, servants shoved her out and locked the door. And in her despair, she followed customs in grieving of the times, tearing her clothes, and covering her lovely hair with ashes. And nothing is mentioned in the story of other women coming to aid with comfort and care; her rapist, too, experienced no penalty for his crime.

I grieve at this unmerited shame. The victim suffers; the attacker doesn't.

"The thief comes only to steal and kill and destroy; I have come that they may have life and have it to the full." [John 10:10]

Jesus' teaching gives two insights. First, this evil was not caused by God or orchestrated by Him. And second, it wasn't caused by me – or you. It comes from "the thief," who the Scripture says is Satan, the Devil, the true Enemy of God and His people. The Bible also calls him "the accuser." Do you know an accuser, someone who is always finding fault, calling out the failings, assigning rotten motives even to good behavior? Multiply that person's impact by a million, and you'll see a taste of the evil Satan intends as he accuses us day and night – to God, to others, and to ourselves. Toxic self-talk, or condemnation from others are his instruments.

The poet and civil rights activist Maya Angelo tells in her autobiography about being raped at age eight by her mother's boyfriend. Charges were filed; he went to prison for a year and a day. Soon after his release, he was found murdered; some speculated he was killed by Maya's uncle. After this event, young Maya concluded that because she spoke up about the assault, *she* was guilty of the man's death. And for the next five years, Maya Angelo didn't speak.

Using her voice cost a person's life; that powerful voice had to be silenced.

What an awful but true picture of the Accuser's work! How pleased he must have been to have dumped a truckload of shame and false guilt on a little child, heavy enough to steal her voice. But the rest of Maya's story and the experiences of other survivors give hope for moving out from under shame and guilt.

To silence shame and false guilt, <u>reject them</u>. I hope this story helps you see the rape was not your fault, not a little, not for a moment. You were, you are not the guilty one. There is no reason to carry shame. So, when these feelings are triggered, either by circumstances or what others might say, shut them out. In your mind and your speech, replace words like "guilty" or "worthless" with Truths like "acceptable," "valuable,' and "innocent."

Second, <u>reclaim the voice God gave you</u>. Maya Angelo's voice came back slowly when a kind teacher introduced her to language she couldn't resist: beautiful poems and inspiring stories, and then asked Maya to read them aloud. As she heard herself in others' words, her own voice awakened. And in the decades to come, that voice would awaken millions of others. So, speak what's true without apology. Every time you do, this truth will become more deeply yours.

Consider forgiveness. And oh, I know from experience that idea may be hard to hear. Maybe even offensive. And I don't suggest it because it's easy, only because God values forgiveness so much. We forgive only because we have been forgiven all our wrongs by the One to whom we owe everything. Sometimes I forgive those who have wronged me because it matters to God or because I've been forgiven so much. Other times I'm moved to offer forgiveness because the price *to me* for holding onto it is so very high, and I'm not willing to give my offender one more inch into my spirit. It may not come this moment, but in your healing, there will come a time when forgiveness will become your doorway to deeper freedom.

And lastly, think about *counseling* as a source of help. A skilled Christian counselor can help you move more quickly from the weariness of shame to a spirit of confidence and release. You are worthy of love. You are worthy of peace, gentleness, and kindness. You are worthy of dignity and belonging. Shame and false guilt were never intended to rule your life; only the God of love and grace deserves that place. So, cry out as the Palmist did, "Do not let me be put to shame, nor let my enemies triumph over me." [Psalm 25:1]

Every time you accept His care to replace shame and guilt, you'll know a deeper touch of *grace over rape*. With that understanding, listen as the writer of the Psalms cries out to God: "Be gracious to me, O Lord, for I am languishing; heal me, O Lord..." [Psalm 6:2] This suffering one is asking for *hen*, that God would care for him as someone the Lord sees as precious, someone of beauty and value. The things we value, we restore. The people we value, we pursue and care for, and invest in. We come for them when they suffer. The writer is saying, "See me as worthy enough to You, Lord, to come for me with comfort and healing and help."

I believe there is a special grace that comes when we are hurting and in need of rescue. It's this special grace the Biblical Apostle Paul refers to when he recounts how God said to him, "My grace is sufficient for you, for my power is made perfect in weakness." [2 Corinthians 12:9]

Nowhere is there a need to receive this kind of power-filled grace than in the case of rape. Circumstances made us too weak to protect ourselves. But God promises to come into this place of need and seek to heal us as ones who are precious and valuable to Him. I have, in times of misery, asked, "Why is this happening to me? Why do I have to suffer in this way?" I've been angry and disappointed with God for what He allowed to happen. But even though the realization may have not come at that moment, I have also been able to see the miracle of grace that I made it through...alive and in my right mind. And often, I've come through with new strength and resources to help another who is traveling the tough road I've walked.

What I have learned is that I have the power to take authority over my thoughts and insecurities. I can speak "life" to myself. I can say to myself, "You are okay; the Lord is with me. He will not leave or forsake me. Remember, we are more than conquerors through Christ Jesus. You Win! The blood of Jesus was shed just for your victory.

Dr. Evelyn Hill

Dr. Evelyn Hill has served on the Kansas City, Kansas Board of Education from July of 2009 through January 2018. During her tenure on the Board of Education, she was the President from July 2014 through July 2017. She values education and believes every child has the right to receive a quality education. She embraces the fact that we are lifetime learners.

Dr. Hill worked with Avenue of Life, a community development organization whose focus is on empowering poor families to become financially self-sufficient with an emphasis on advocating for families who have been challenged with judicial systems and beyond.

Dr. Hill has worked strategically with Avenue of Life, KCK School District, and other agencies to decrease the number of homeless kids in the school district. The original number of 1400 homeless kids have decreased by over 50%.

Since the death of George Floyd and other African American civilians in 2020, along with the COVID-19 pandemic, Dr. Hill has been moved to speak up for the under-served communities in our metropolitan areas around the country.

Dr. Hill has been a pastor and servant leader in the community. She co-founded the Wyandotte County Justice and Equity Coalition in Wyandotte County.

Dr. Hill enjoys public speaking, group training, and facilitation. Dr. Hill is very passionate about empowering women and children through education. Dr. Hill is also very passionate about the civil rights of all humans. Justice issues must move from talk to action that frees the innocent and oppressed. Justice must meet the requirement of "being just and fair" and value the life of all humans.

Connect with Dr. Evelyn

Website: www.drevelynhill.net

Campaign page: www.drhill4kck.com

Facebook page: www.facebook.com/DrEvelynHill

Linkedin Page: https://www.linkedin.com/in/dr-evelyn-hill-100a0112/

Overcoming Adversity
By Kellie Knights

Most of my decisions were contingent upon concealing experiences I endured in my youth! Having encountered so much confusion and trauma, I was led by poor behaviors, suffering much strife, abandonment, and loneliness. My youth had been robbed; my teenage years were scrambled. Selfish, out of control, and blatantly disregarding reverence for anyone, I did not fear consequences because no one gave me a reason to. Year after year, I was this lost and lonely little girl who had to figure it out alone. Although I did not finish high school, I was smart enough to survive.

I had a passion for education, always learning, and set out to rise above my current conditions. I insisted on trying to rebuild severely broken relationships because I was empty with no purpose, leadership, or guidance. These familiar people I already perceived couldn't help me except remind me of deep pain and agony that yearned to be filled with unconditional love. What exactly did I expect from them? Someone who would support me emotionally and be attentive to my desires. Someone who would give me a reason to be driven, but that fulfillment never happened!

As I continued in my young adult years on the run in search of my purpose, I always wanted things to work in my favor but often got caught up showing up for everyone else's events. I was maintaining normal living activities, just existing, forging happiness and contentment. Sure, among many people, I was revered and admired! To others, I was mysterious and misunderstood so much that assumptions about me led them to pretentious actions. My true self was hidden. There was an inner me that was yet to be revealed. My current position was outside the alignment of who I was destined to be, and I knew this because I was always uncomfortable! There was lucid change needed, and it required action.

As much as I had endured, it still didn't suffice who I was! I hadn't even begun to thrive. I witnessed people allow adversity to stimulate their aspirations into keeping busy and stressing their bodies out or flat out live in oblivion and, unfortunately, develop underlying health issues. They either failed to manage their physical health, or their soul would carry the weight of heavy burdens of guilt, shame, and self-pity. Neither way suited me since it would only reflect my mental stability.

Yes, I had pushed through obstacles and maintained my sanity, but it was not enough to check off as absolute amazement. Of course, I had encountered many amazing mentions, transformations & wows, mainly to me, because only I knew my back story. I profusely reminded myself I was not mediocre and there must be more to my story. There was vague evidence of success. There were not many highlights I could easily reflect on. It was difficult to remember events that I could say were *a time to remember*! With my mind constantly cluttered with burdens of adversity, I just got tired of the same old story resurfacing my hardships, the old thoughts of what could've, would've, or should've been. Recollecting the "oh woe is me, moments," I was sharp in acknowledging what I didn't have and who I didn't have. This was the cliche of my life.

Staringly gazing beyond the stars, my imagination wandered to create my life! To finally tell my story unashamed, from surviving to thriving! What does the ending of my book look like? What was the grand mission I needed to accomplish? What was the end goal? What was the plan to achieve said goals? How was I going to make great things happen?

Prioritizing my battles was a matter of planning and strategizing necessary methods to choose my needs. To tackle the challenges that would stretch me out of comfort by encountering the hard stuff, to work out the most important actions to increase healing and wellness. Wrestling often with the depths of what I had overcome and people's thoughts of my past kept me on edge. Not too much because I considered what they said, but telling my truth was relevant to my success story. It was imperative to accept the reality of everyone having opinions. However, I was responsible for controlling my outcome! Being defeated was not even a question.

I needed to stop running and unleash what was deeply rooted in me, waiting to be revealed! With reckoning my options, I had to pursue my

PRIORITIZING MY BATTLES

business with intention! It was a matter of prioritizing what was most important for advancing and improving my situation. Redeeming my reputation was a priority. While in a state of rebellion and disobedience, I even developed a background with the law and had been in relationships that needed to be renounced! I was limited in making the traditional moves, but by grace, I had a favor. No More being blind and used by unbelief or fear. I needed to refresh and understand the value of who I was and identify my true capabilities of exceeding excellence and beyond my observation!

    In wisdom, I learned to use this same blindness or lack of support as self-determination. I began to comprehend that I had power; the light switched on, and suddenly, I had foresight of my future! My vision had changed. It needed to be clear, and it needed to be prominent to me for execution! I wanted to make great things happen! I wanted to overcome my battles but remained uncertain of my purpose! I needed a change because even while aging, my mind remained immature, and that lost little girl would resurface as it reflected how deprived I truly was!

Most of my decisions felt like regret. I unknowingly made decisions that cost me long-term experiences impacting my future, whether good or bad. I had to learn to live with them. I needed to allow the breaking up and separation from agreements. I had to disconnect from self-sabotage and anything that did not serve my needs or add value to my new self-discovery! It was time I realized my wants and needs were *mine*. So, when choosing me, I needed to prioritize my emotions, beliefs, and the people I allow in my space!

Creating boundaries was a practice I needed to implement to get well! Releasing from generational traditions and unlearning everything I ever knew. I needed direction or a teacher who defined life without bias and purity. With redirecting my focus and intentions toward discovering myself, connecting with new and unfamiliar people was a priority. I would always advocate for others but never for myself. I could sharply give suggestions and advice based on the discussion and provide options and resources subject to my own experiences, but I learned that I was trauma bonding most times.

I am profusely emptying tears that were full from being held back, always trying to be strong because I relate to others and pour way too much, connecting to their pain. The whole time, I thought I could help save others; I needed the help. I needed to save myself. I needed to keep from drowning myself with false initiatives and take the initiative to tackle the necessary objectives that were so prevalent in changing my mind. I needed to be the face of resilience and overcome this adversity that aggressively had me in a chokehold, always being the headline of my story.

We're all familiar with the statement, "Life is like a roller coaster. There are a lot of ups and downs," In the rollercoaster experience, we decide to endure the whole process! We anticipate the adrenaline of the roller coaster, preparing for the enjoyment of the ride to highlight the thrill of it all! The ups and downs, the excitement and discomfort, we mutually agree to be caught up in the moment!

Having confidence and courage was required for the due process, and that concluded the full performance. Life's battles are no different. Battles are not always physically seen or head-on obstacles. The majority of our battles are unforeseen. Behind the scenes, which we define as spiritual battles where shifts happen surrounding positive or negative influences, and how we respond will determine the outcome. Who we are connected to also has its merits; your daily routines and activities, what you adhere to, by way of hearing, and what you watch all impact your thoughts and actions!

    Then something happened, and I realized it was necessary to redirect my attention to improve my mental wellness, from deprivation and refocus. I needed to prioritize my beliefs. I needed to stop making excuses and take control. I needed to stop resisting the future me. It was time I stopped blaming my past mishaps and misfortunes for the lack of my success! I was the answer! I was the solution. I needed to listen to that small, quiet voice and believe I was great. My source was with me this whole time. Storms and distractions will come, but you must stay strong and focused until execution. With much self-talk on finishing the mission, you must keep your word and finish what you started. I couldn't afford to keep fighting

myself. It was time until the next chapter of my life was revealed! By grace, all things will abound!
-AN OVERCOMER OF ADVERSITY!

Kellie Knights

Kellie Knights is a multicultural millennial and mompreneur constantly evolving, pushing through and assuring her story's testimony reaches the body of people intended! Kellie is a multi-talented creative fashion enthusiast, speaker, advocate, and now author, always excelling to take on challenges that will achieve excellence! She is known for getting to the root and removing the veil of the unknown. Kellie gives her narrative in this anthology," Prioritizing My Battles."

Email: smeminentvirtue@gmail.com
Facebook: Kellie Knights
IG: Nolimit_2Modest

Walking Wounded
By Muriah Brown

On May 25, 1960, an angel was born by the name of Linda Marie Curry. Linda was a mother of two. Linda struggled with substance abuse for 30 years of her life. In December 2020, she decided she was done with drugs, so she checked herself into rehab and remained sober.

In July of 2022, Linda was diagnosed with stage four colon cancer. Initially, chemotherapy seemed to be working, tumors were shrinking, and faith was rising. In May of 2023, cancer started to grow rapidly. In July of 2023, Linda was hospitalized for over a month, and she lost her mobility. In August, she was discharged from the hospital and moved to Indiana to be closer to her daughter and grandchildren. Her daughter began to care for her, which only lasted a week and a half before she had to be hospitalized again. This time...she was never discharged. She passed away on October 7, 2023, at 8:40 A.M.

Linda is my mother, my best friend and confidant. Caring for her and praying for her was my life. I would work 60 hours a week, take care of my two children, attend school online, and care for my mother. I did it with joy, and would have done it for the rest of my life if given the opportunity. While I cared for my mother, I tried desperately to increase her faith. I made post-it notes with bible scriptures and put them throughout my home. In places she frequented. I would pray daily that God would give me something to encourage her, to strengthen her. As her health began to decline, I would ask God why he had me 300 miles away, I would travel back and forth each weekend, and it was truly exhausting.

God told me one day that she needed to learn to depend on me, not you. You are not God. I understood, but it did not make things easier. I continued to ask God to move her closer to me, and God delivered. He allowed me to bring her home. As I cared for her, some days, she would weep and tell me how strong I was. I would tell her that it was not me; it was all God. What great joy I received from serving and taking care of her. Would have done it for the rest of my life if I had to. I have no regrets. I can't think of a time when she needed me and I was not there. I loved her dearly and honored her as my mom.

Somedays, it was hard to show up in the world without resentment and bitterness. I began to neglect some of my responsibilities and commitments. My grades began to fail in school; work was becoming unmanageable. Things I committed myself to, I immediately withdrew from without notice. I thought I had the right to not show up because I was hurting; I was dealing with a lot. One day God told me that I had no right to play the victim, I had no right to stop showing up like I was supposed to...I was walking wounded. When we are walking wounded, we think we have a past to not be the people God created us to be. We think we have the right to be rude, to not minister, to not pray for others. I admit I was self, and family-absorbed.

All I wanted to do was say, "What about me?" Or "Do you know what I'm going through?" I had to get over myself. The reality is that life goes on, and we still must show up, with a broken heart, with all our wounds. I am reminded of the Peter and the boat experience as I think about walking wounded. Every time I shifted focus from God, I began to drown. God showed me how and why I should break the victim mentality.

As God was correcting me, he brought Luke 22:42-44. Jesus wrestled with anxiety from the cup he was given by the Father. Jesus asked God to remove this cup from him, "But nevertheless, your will be done." I prayed relentlessly, day and night, asking that God heal my mother. My faith was strong. Even when doctors tried bullying me into deciding to pull the plug on my mom, I stood firm in my faith that God was going to heal her, but nevertheless, let your will be done, God.

Each day, I showed up to the hospital, most days, twice a day. I prayed over her; I prophesied over her. Each time I pulled up, anxiety hit me like a ton of bricks. I did not want to be there; my flesh was weak and afraid. God continued to strengthen me. 2 Corinthians 12:9; his strength was made perfect in my weakness. The Lord gave me a word; he promised beautiful healing. My flesh thought it meant that there was no way my mom would pass away, but my spirit recognized that God can and will heal supernaturally, and there will be a beautiful rainbow at the end of this storm. Every time we make it through a tough trial, we won't get the support we feel we should get.

Walking wounded is my journey and testimony. I'm sure plenty of readers can identify with some of the feelings I have gone through. When life gets challenging, we shut off the world and press into the pain instead of pressing into our Father, not realizing that through the testing, we find God's hand. Although I didn't get the outcome I wanted, my mother healed on earth; I am at peace. I promised God that no matter the outcome, you will get the glory.

This season has been lonely for me. God isolated me from friends and from family, so I had only him to lean on. I know that God is working all things out for me. He is pruning me and maturing me in my faith and into the person he created me to be, and for that, I have great joy.

When you are chosen by God, you don't get to neglect your calling. Heartbreaking moments are a part of the journey, and God will use each moment for his glory. God will use everything the enemy sent to destroy us, to prune us, to mature us in him. He is working all things out for our good. So, the next time you are wounded, keep walking and don't look down!

This chapter is dedicated to my beautiful mother, Linda Curry-Clark. You are truly missed.

PRIORITIZING MY BATTLES

Muriah Brown

Muriah Brown was brown and raised in St. Louis, Mo. Muriah is currently attending school at Indiana Wesylan University, pursuing a degree in Social Work. Muriah is the mother of two amazing children. Muriah has created an organization, Pretty People Promoting Positivity, in hopes of encouraging young women to live life abundantly, urbanizing certain stories of those who may be confused. Muriah is very excited to be a part of the Anthology.

Connect with Muriah Brown
FB: muriah.brown.54

Made in the USA
Monee, IL
05 November 2023